BENCHES

BENCHES

Peggy Jones

ISBN: 978-1-9996239-1-3

Copy edited by Ian Large

Cover design by Jag Lall

All photographs from the author's personal collection

This book is produced by Peggy Jones Publishing in conjunction with WRITERSWORLD, and is produced entirely in the UK. It is available to order from most bookshops in the United Kingdom, and is also globally available via UK based Internet book retailers.

WRITERSWORLD
2 Bear Close Flats, Bear Close, Woodstock
Oxfordshire, OX20 1JX, England
☎ 01993 812500
☎ +44 1993 812500

www.writersworld.co.uk

The text pages of this book are produced via an independent certification process that ensures the trees from which the paper is produced come from well managed sources that exclude the risk of using illegally logged timber while leaving options to use post-consumer recycled paper as well.

For John

There is never an end to loss or hope
I give up the ghost for which I grope
Over and over again saying, Amen
To all that has and hasn't happened
The eternal event is now not when

(Samuel Menashe, *Now*)

Contents

Book I

Introduction

I have explored ways of structuring *Benches* that allow the original writings their own space whilst providing a separate space for reflections that require – and required – a very different sort of attention, presence, and participation. The writings that follow, in Book I, are 'rough', unedited. They appear here as they appear in my notebooks. I have gathered them into sections: 'Benches', 'Moments', 'Words', 'Hard, Bitter Things', 'Iconography', 'Time and Tide', 'Healing', 'Return', and 'Kaleidoscope'. In some cases, there is a quotation or a brief introduction to the section itself.

The latter writings have been revised, discarded, retrieved, and re-explored; they are gathered into parallel sections in Book II. Between most of these sections I have inserted a narrative – in seven 'Parts' – reviewing the long process of me and *Benches* coming together. The arrangement I settled on recognises, I hope, the interweaving of, and connectedness between, quite different 'voices' and moods, but doesn't attempt to blend them artificially.

I have chosen 'Rough Edges' to introduce both Book I and Book II.

Rough Edges

My mother had a way of walking on a beach that I (and my siblings) learned to imitate from a young age. At the tide line or where the waves were just washing in, she would walk slowly, head bent, scanning the sand – not looking for anything in particular, just scanning, seeing what caught her eye: beach-combing. Occasionally she would bend down and pick something up, look at it, perhaps brush some grains of sand off it if it was a shell, or lick it, if it was a piece of sea glass, to see what it looked like wet. Most of what was picked up was tossed back down again, but a few bits were casually, almost unconsciously, slipped into a pocket as she continued walking. As children we treasured sea glass most highly, and the very best pieces were blue, or the oh-so-rare red ones that we occasionally found. But there was one inflexible rule to be applied: if the edges were still at all rough or sharp, it was not considered to be legitimately 'sea glass' – not yet. This rule was accepted and applied rigorously by all of us, to our own treasures and to each other's – the decision was beyond dispute.

Rough Edges

Not smoothing my words
or their rhythms: they're
not like sea glass,
washed and washed, bleached
and ground down
under the sun
under the moon.
If I could do that
I wouldn't need to do this.
Instead, they are rough-edged
like the grains of sand
that polish the glass
making it soft, worn,
beautiful,
a thing of time,
almost alive.

Benches

Whether occupied or unoccupied, new or broken, large or small, wet or dry, the nature of a bench remains unchanged: it is silent, empty – like a teacup waiting to serve its purpose – neutral, useful, never used up.

12 slats make the back
5, thicker, longer, the seat
Emptiness, the bench

Benches

Given By
John and Marjorie Ruck
In Gratitude for Kew Gardens

Clouds of soft lilac rhododendron
birdsong
grasses and buttercups
peacock calls
mown paths – kindly inviting –
and this bench with beautiful
pale green and grey papery islands of lichen
between and on the slats
edges curled up or lying flat
like snowflakes – spread out.
A home for the moss, too.
The bench the Rucks gave in gratitude
is being gratefully colonized
by Kew Gardens, in one of its
miniature forms.
And long waving purple seed-heads sway alongside me
or push through the back slabs.
So many different grasses.

I thought: it's not that I want
to capture the moment,
leave alone, create a moment;
it's something more like
acknowledging or witnessing

or being alive in this moment
and the moment already past
when a squirrel passed from
the path into the long grass,
long gone, now.

The sun disappeared
and my winter arms –
bared for a few minutes –
are now re-covered;
my light duvet coat and my scarf
are reclaimed.

A bee investigates me –
around my lips –
a quick glimpse of my face –
Gone
And I, too, am so grateful to Kew Gardens!

~

Essus Tock
1894-1983
Man of the Countryside
Greatly Loved

~

Too wet to sit on
and yet – I do –
on this grey damp cold
last day of February

A coal tit – bird feeders
snowdrops
the charcoal burners' path

I picked a dry and
twisting beech leaf –
you haven't seen a thing
until you've drawn it –

I am wild and rushing inside
needing benches and beech leaves
even mud
and a coal tit – birdsong:
a robin: 'The feeders are empty!'

$\sim$

I sit on a bench for 'Vigo',
who died aged 24:
'Meet me down on the bank of the beautiful river
when your journey has end. Love you.'

$\sim$

The bench I sit on
is nameless, anonymous.
I call it, 'Right Now'.

Eyes closed, I listen:
voices, footsteps, gulls, planes, geese.
'Right Now' is my anchor.

Eyes opened, I blink,
blue, wind-blown, shining river,
and hunched young heron.

~

Benches with no backs
are more demanding, but still
they suggest a pause.

~

The dew-dropped grass
in front of my bench
(In Loving Memory of
Dr. Bolko Hagen
(1924-2003))
is be-jewelled:
tiny brilliant lights
sparkle – gold, green, blue
gems of living light
hundreds and hundreds
and hundreds

still-wet grasses
like Christmas trees
red, gold, green
ruby, topaz, emerald
tiny testaments to
earth-shattering
beauty
amber and diamonds,
sapphires
tiny, brilliant, transient
thousands and thousands
galaxies of pinpricks of light –
at my feet
suns and moon and nebulae
tiny, radiant
sun-given.
    Thanks.

~

A bench to Freg Hutt
'Jabba the Pizza'
died at 39 – a big heart
I guess –
his bench – by the lock –
is garnished with lavender
ever-lasting flowers
tied with a shiny lavender bow.
The water rushes through the lock.

~

SAM K. PASTAKIA 1931 – 2001
A man of love, gentleness and charity – eternally loved
by family and friends

~

Everything passes and vanishes
Everything leaves its trace;
And often you see in a footstep
What you could not see in a face.
Philip Hector Barnard
1917 – 2004

In faces, in bodies, in moments
seeing something else – Other –
another dimension to a person
a moment
a landscape
a thought
something parts or opens, or dissolves –
solidity dissolves
the solidity of anything – everything –
this bench: here now, not in 2003
when Philip Hector Barnard
was still alive.
Me – a coming together and
then a release of what came together –
'Everything leaves its trace.'

Does it? Or is it just for we humans –
cells and molecules, yes,
but anything more?
An alteration in the pattern –
almost invisible – the patterning –
no such thing as moments –
that's only about our measurement of Time –
It's seamless – like Priestley's vision
indivisible
death always in us, happening,
life always in us, happening –

~

Finding a spot to sit
isn't always easy –
plenty of choice – that's not the problem –
it's: who am I today?
Where do I fit in?
I look for yesterday's bench
with yesterday's thoughts
and ideas
and my feet swerve off
in another direction,
so I let go and see where they take me –
I realize how tired I am;
my body tells me
to lower my expectations
of now,
to be content with sun and breeze

and cloud
and endlessly diverse – and unsketchable –
greenery;

the yin and yang of how things grow –
pushing forward or upward
yielding, digging into the ground
or seeking shade,
rather than sun

each so different, so beautiful
shaded bed of hydrangeas
summer-faded, rose-coloured heads

and every dedicated bench
carrying its message of love
and gratitude
to a no longer present, but always dear, one (or ones)
and to an endlessly generous and bountiful
Kew Gardens

Thanks from me, too,
and love to all my dear ones
– with us or gone –

~

Stephen Kingsley
1948 – 2002
A caring and thoughtful man of great courage

In the Cemetery

So much love
So much sadness
So much beauty
Youth and age
'Lived one day'
'Beloved eldest son'
A sunburst or comet of gold
'born of the Spirit – cannot die –
Mother of 3 – final radiance'.

I change benches on account of the rain
and find Alex's grave.
A brave little boy – aged 9.
A photo of a serious and bright-eyed child:
'For Alex who fought and lost but enriched many lives
along the way.'
The newness of death in this corner.

~

Grove Road Cemetery

Odd flopped gravestones
Lichen-covered sad – or praying, or triumphant –
angels
with sad – or inflight – wings.

I am crooked and sad and in mourning
and prayerful and triumphant, too,
so, I find myself here –
alienated by the crosses –
or maybe just puzzled –
An autumn afternoon –
almost warm.
Ground shifts topple monuments
or nudge them to one side or another.
The pensive angel holding her trumpet (or his)
must surely have once been upright –
and not on Emily Schofield's smooth
even austere
dark granite resting place.

But Time is here, reminding me,
in obliterated writing
and tumbled stone work,
of what nature does naturally:
move and alter and erode and create.

I don't know why I find myself here
or who I find
or where –

~

Paul Mossop
Oct 1965 – Oct 1999
'My lovely son'

Those who won't be feeling this wind,
hearing these birds –
all the 'lovely' ones – beloved,
missed, thought about each October.

Moments

And some time make the time to drive out west
Into County Clare, along the Flaggy Shore,
In September or October, when the wind
And the light are working off each other
So that the ocean on one side is wild
With foam and glitter, and inland among the stones
The surface of a slate-grey lake is lit
By the earthed lightning of a flock of swans
Their feathers roughed and ruffling, white on white,
Their fully grown headstrong-looking heads
Tucked or cresting or busy underwater.
Useless to think you'll park and capture it
More thoroughly. You are neither here nor there,
A hurry through which known and strange things pass
As big soft buffetings come at the car sideways
And catch the heart off guard and blow it open.

(Seamus Heaney[1])

---

[1] Heaney, Seamus, p,70

Moments

Miso Soup Medicine

This – the totality of it –
No labels,
No this or that
All – the gestalt –
so much greater than the sum of its parts,
Indivisible
Not that parts can't be named:
November
gusty
fast flowing Thames
afternoon
clouds over sun
seagulls – airborne, water-borne –
bridge
cars
hot miso soup

and if I try to describe one thing –
the water – it would fill all the books
in the world,
and it still would not be
this water
Now,
as the light and the wind
and the gulls
play over it –
'working off each other'

or
this bird
the one that just banked and
swooped over there
and now drifts downstream
backwards
with 7 others
or
these clouds
all water and light, glancing
then diffuse
complicated by the wind
or
this November
or those people
trudging over Richmond Bridge
heads down
as the buses and cars pass
or
this miso soup
or

* * * * *

The flow of the river here
Now
the man raking bright, wet plane tree leaves
the gulls squalling, the sun – glancing onto the brown river
which flows fast now,
towards the sea

The cormorant, just glimpsed, by the bank –
bright omen of the Present –
dips and disappears into a
flowing patch of sunlight,
sparkling.

* * * * *

By the bridge – <u>this</u> bridge
with its radiant arches –
muddy Thames water flows,
a crow bends his wing
cuts the air past me –
my coffee finished
(to the last chocolatey drop)
plane tree leaves, now brown and dry
and others, still green and yellow,
hang softly against a grey sky.
The crow swoops again...
but it feels like a waiting space;
the tide flows out – emptying –
gulls drift lazily
and the crow flies past again –
under an arch
above the water.
What is this?
Another leaf falls.

* * * * *

It is a grey, foggy day
in London (town),
but it doesn't have me low or down.
I quite like it
even the cold drip that just fell
from the tree onto the green
plastic
chair
next to me.

And I'm the old lady
in the pink hat and scarf
who wiped her chair
with a Kleenex
and then sat on her shopping bag.

* * * * *

Not Miso Soup but
Moroccan Date and Pecan Cake,
and I'm back by the bridge
with the wind and the sky
and the water
'working off each other' –
thank you, Seamus.
Blossom and that amazing green haze
that is not-yet-leaf –
it must have a name.
The wind blows my hair
and the pigeons and jackdaws
stalk each crumb
that might blow off a plate,
or fall from my fingers.
And we can't believe what has come to pass –
Is this really the same world
we were inhabiting yesterday?
A tiny insect flew into my tea –
I fished it out,
but I fear the tea was too hot –
Now he dries, feet in the air,

on the edge of my plate
...and I am here feeling
blessed by wind and water
and Seamus Heaney,
and the day has been a good one
(except for the insect).

* * * * *

I have 2,290 miles to go
(the Moving Map tells me)
The sky, ringed with a halo of
wispy, disappearing peach and apricot
light, deepest, oceanic, blue
and where it meets the peach, whispers
into a blue so crystalline, so pure
you could drink it –
the sky tells me I have a universe
to breathe, to be –
I am not of this earth up here
(at 34,000 pieds)
well, I am tethered, as a boat is
on a mooring.
Beneath me the cloud is present and dark,
and darkening.
There – a star (or Venus, more likely)
and on my wingtip – my star – my light,
as I travel into night
above a planet that turns and turns
and gives me 2 hours of sunset.

But I'm not travelling fast enough –
it isn't 'into night' that I am travelling –
it's a race to stay ahead of night,
and it's winning.

＊ ＊ ＊ ＊ ＊

(Logan Airport)
An hour to go
An apricot sky over what must be Boston
but looks unreal behind airport glass.

The sky is peach
I finished my Codewords
and sit with another glass of red.
Businessman, pregnant lady with a little blonde toddler –
She's pushing a pushchair and pulling a suitcase,
and I bet she's tired. I am.

The sky is pink and mauve
No plane announcements –
quiet, very pleasant,
but disconcerting –
I must pay attention –

The sky is baroque –
pink and orange and streaky fuchsia,
and I wonder if that man
facing me
even knows what is
growing and spreading behind his back,

outside the window –
a wine-red sky,
a fairy-tale, other-world sky.

* * * * *

On the Terrace, sun behind low grey and apricot clouds
the river silvery shiny, but uninviting,
the wind making me and others button our collars –
photo-takers line up a view: of the scene, of each other, or – if
somebody offers –
of themselves in front of the view;
kids' voices...
It feels like one of the last evenings we can do this –
Before it's too chilly, too dark –
But oh! The sun bottoms out of the grey cloud
Bathing us all in golden apricot.
It takes your breath away –
The wake of a boat is shot-silk
a couple embrace
I am blinded by gold – will it stay? On this page –
Will I see it when I next read what I have written?
Moments – words or photos – we are all trying to capture
them, as they fly away –
I'm eating pumpkin seeds which I roasted in honour of
Halkidiki –
will taste help me remember?
People are just silhouettes against a gold and airplane-blue
backdrop –
Friends, lovers, fathers and sons,

A man on a bike with his kid behind, lost under a helmet –
This moment, Now.
iPads: everybody can turn and try to capture this moment of
evening and wind
of grey and cold and oncoming darkness
bathed in gold –

　　　　* * * * *

Into the woods where I saw...
the gently blowing patterns of
shadowy leaves thrown onto the screen of
the chestnut tree next to me.
Contingency:
this moment it is happening;
this moment I'm sitting here to see it –
the sun shining through those leaves;
for a few minutes casting a shadow
of twig and leaf –
and then the sun has moved,
falling elsewhere through the woods,
doing other remarkable,
unremarked things.

　　　　* * * * *

I felt as I looked at the pond, or saw the pond –
how everything passes – moves and passes.
Life is just this wind, this light,
never still, always changing.
Of course, there will be terrible loss,

but it is just the wind and the light
passing, moving, alive –
this is life – alive, moving –
and everything passing, always, and
arising.

* * * * *

The sweetness of this air
almost makes me drunk
coming in the dark door
full of water and freshness
full of scents of something
unknown and intoxicating

* * * * *

Dappling – that's what life is
 – light and shadow –
always moving and changing
through the 'leaves' that we are...
each person a dapple
 – a shifting thing –
now light, now shadow, indecipherable
now perhaps moving on
  – the light has moved on –
I know nothing.

* * * * *

There is something about the moment
this moment
here and gone
as close to its source as we can get
just emerging from the Dark
as close to the source –
the Tao
the singularity
where space and time start
almost without qualities –
without qualities –
a first translucent bead
unmade, just emerging
Is this what I felt about contingency?
So the emergent no-thing becomes a thing when there are
conditions,
when it is conditioned
So maybe Miso Soup Medicine is about tracking the no-thing
of the emergent moment
through its manifestations,
which are infinite –

　　　　* * * * *

In the end it turns out to be so incredibly simple
and light:
the wind on the pond
the night-dark door
and its gift, its invitation...
This morning, the moving shadows of chestnut leaves –

in a shadowed wood,
the canvas of a tree trunk
holds the dancing form of a 5-fingered chestnut leaf
passing, as it moves,
Now long gone, as I sip my coffee in Kew.

* * * * *

So simple, the contingency of me in that wood, at that
moment,
as the sun streamed through
a gap in the trees,
the breeze touched the leaves of that tree
and I saw
(because at that moment
I was not looking elsewhere,
or too absorbed in my thoughts to notice)
a dancing shadow.

Always it is like that,
the lightness of contingency
the lightness of the passing moments.

* * * * *

The peacock
standing on one side of the path,
His tail covered the path to the other side –
stopped me in my tracks
(in my walking meditation)
– miraculous, unbelievable, inconceivable

I greeted him admiringly –
he slowly spread and raised his
astonishing tail,
rustled his strong under-feathers
to sound like a drum-roll,
and then turned and turned.
Then he opened his prehistoric beak
and cracked open the air.
Everything glowed and shimmered
and shimmied in the sun...
and all words fail.

Words

1.

'The fish weir is the means to arrest a fish. Once one has caught the fish, one forgets about the fish weir. The snare is the means to arrest a hare. Once one has caught the hare, one forgets about the snare. Spoken words are the means to arrest a thought. Once one has caught the thinking, one forgets about the words. Where will I find a man who forgets about words to talk with him?' [2]

2.

'To make deer-hunting medicine, first you learn to see the bush that's in front of you, then the bush behind that bush, then the deer behind the bush behind the bush that's in front of you, then the spirit of that deer. Now you can call the deer, his spirit, and he'll walk up to you.' [3]

---

[2]   Wagner, Rudolph G., p. 32

[3]   eds. D. M. Dooling and Paul Jordan-Smith, p. 52

Words

1.
the fish-weir

First you observe the water,
how it flows, where deep, where shallow
where shady, where flowing in dappled
shadow and sun.
First, you listen to it, in summer
in winter, in flood-times
and drought.
First you allow your skin to be
that of the fish, to feel how
the currents flow, how the
weeds or the rocks caress
or graze the skin.
First you see the sun rise over the water,
the moonshine speckling each tiny ripple;
you look at the stars from below
the water
you feel the pulse and the pound
of the rainstorm.
Then, if you can bear it,
you imagine where you would lie
or jump
(your fish-self, that is) –
what might lure you
into particular waters
(which might conceal a weir)
You try not to allow your fish-self

to feel the panic and pain
of entrapment
because, if you did
you wouldn't be able
to do it.

2.

deer-hunting medicine/the second bush

The first is, perhaps, a more
gross purification,
a first emptying
(which must be repeated
and repeated):
wants, wishes, desires, fears,
preconceptions, narratives,
ideas of gain or triumph.
The second is, perhaps, a much
greater refinement,
through waiting,
patience,
not waiting <u>for</u> something,
maybe waiting <u>on</u> something,
a stillness,
and a calling,
(an invocation – a prayer)
So when we say
"Deer" or
"Fish", we might as well be saying
"God", since there is nothing
greater than that which we wait upon.
We sit in the spirit;
We call or sing or cry from the spirit;
we wait on the spirit
of the deer
or the fish

to reveal itself,
to come to us.
We must not lunge towards it
or seek to trick or trap or snare it.
(That might catch the flesh but never the spirit.)
And when we sit with things in this way,
without hope or expectations
(but maybe with love, even longing)
they may reveal themselves to us,
then maybe we might see the Other,
then maybe they might come to us,
then maybe we might come together
in light, a communion,
a joining.

And so I see the Second bush is
death
and there are many types of
death:
the death of a snowflake
or a dream
or a life.
Well, maybe they're all the same
as light as the
feather against which the
soul was weighed at the Egyptian
moment of death.
To be as weightless as a snowflake
or a feather –
no attachment to heart or muscle

to birdsong
or nest
or flight –
to not know that earlier state,
or not regret it.

* * * * *

'Today, here amongst the trees and frosted leaves
and glancing, pure winter sunshine,
the familiar sounds of birds and children,
voices in the distance – and airplanes –
I looked to see where I would walk or sit.
I looked and saw the familiar scene –
then I looked again
at the trees
and saw, instead,
their patience,
their eagerness to meet my searching eyes,
their readiness to leap towards me,
now recognized.

(later: 'I believe the "natural" world is, like the deer, always "present", in this sense, ready to leap towards us, to offer us its grace and beauty and blessing. It is up to us whether we choose to stop and sit still long enough – and with love enough – to see it.')

* * * * *

'The bush and I are one; there is no second bush.'

Hard, Bitter Things

I asked myself: what is my place in all this?
And then felt my stone-like chest – tight, constricted, hard –
a heavy heart; I carry a heavy heart –
and maybe that's my place, my part,
for today,
and if I am inseparable from the whole, then I carry that
heavy heart
for us all, because as much as it is good in every way to have
a light heart, often (for humans, at least) we carry a heavy
heart.
Yesterday, after my coffee, I walked and saw they are draining
the Thames,
opening the sluices, letting it all flow naturally,
scouring the riverbed – a sort of cleansing –
and there was the cormorant I'd been looking for –
a bob, an alert glance around,
and down he popped again –
an opportunity for him: less water means more fish in what
remains –
is there a moral here? No.
The Canada geese honk out their stories of territory and
bonding
just as the stags do –
the sky turns greyer; the wind is up, here by Pen Ponds.
Life never stops (the cormorant embodies that truth in all his
eager energy).
The gulls swoop in a cloud at the other side of the pond.

Green and gold sweet chestnut leaves quiver in the wind –
loving kindness is often translated from the Pali as 'the quivering
of the heart' – a heavy heart is a greater weight for the winds of life
to set a-quiver;
and it returns to its resting place
more quickly, gravity winning the day.

Heavy thoughts, but a somewhat lighter heart? Not sure –
Let it be; let it be; let it be.

* * * * *

Feeling in need of something –
some comfort –
The hard, bitter seeds and skins of the grapes I just bought,
the hard bitter thing in my chest...
The cormorant's dip and dive and energy lift me –
for a moment –
but then the fatigue
and the brown river
and the grey sky
reclaim me
and I am alienated from Christmas and
the people I smile at
as they pass.

I guess I am trying to fashion
a fish-weir here,
to sift the Tao fish
out of the muddy 'Thames',
as the cormorant does –
making a meal of it.

(I tried a few haiku which helped – I liked the pun!)

Building a fish-weir
to catch the quick, gloomy fish
(as cormorants do)

I'm fishing for food
in ebbing muddy waters
and making a meal of it

* * * * *

I just keep falling
into a me that seems to be terrified
and keeps backing away from something,
trying to make the world
smaller and more manageable,
so I can feel its edges
and know its limits.
But the problem is, I shrink
and back up against some wall
which is too close and my space-time becomes too small
and I am gasping
and more terrified

because all my instincts
seem to be wrong,
to lead me to the smaller
and the more tightly controlled
when what I really need
is space and freedom and light.

* * * * *

There is more,
something more –
some outrage about
death, about moving towards it
about being seen to be moving
towards it –
almost like shame –
to be so visible
so visibly on that path
that others
know it, take it for granted;
(I hear Mum say to me,
outrage in her voice:
'You're not the one who is dying.')
How dare anybody else
know I am on that path –
how dare they think about the time when
I am dead,
or even think about
me dying?
It is so private, so personal, so

intimate a thing to imagine
about me –
so terrible a thing
to intrude upon
to presume upon
Indignity upon indignity,
unbearable
almost
unbearable.

* * * * *

Rain and rain and rain
and I feel
so low.
Where is the point of
balance
that allows all this
to slip into place,
to become background –
when it is all there is,
it is neither weir nor fish,
neither bush nor deer.
Rain Medicine – what does it teach?
To fall, when fall you must,
no matter how it affects lives –
drowning some
slaking the thirst of others
washing away
houses and hopes.

The football continues –
muddy men and boys.
My head throbs.
Why this?
Because.

* * * * *

Marathon

A Chechen – Judas – chosen by karma.
It lands on him and he also cannot
'let this cup pass'
any more than Jesus could –
2 sides of one coin –
If there is a Jesus
there will also be a Judas
and neither will have chosen their paths,
their roles – yet both are necessary.
So – a 19 year old boy –
more an American than a Chechen –
and he is the scapegoat for all of us –
we can blame him, tie our burdens
on his back and get rid of him
(one way or another).
His older brother – the more angry,
it would seem,
the more friendless –
is dead, and this one must answer
for him, too, and for all Muslims,
and for the hate and confusion and

impotence and fear
which we all feel.
For a brief moment it will be
'All his fault'.
He will have to suffer more
for us, because we must not be implicated;
it must be one young man –
this young man –
who carries our cross,
who is the Christ, in this passion play –
although his name is Judas, in this passion play –
although his name is Chechen –
unpronounceable, impossible to remember
in this passion play.
He is Everyman; he is all of us;
he is the threshold, the doorway
we must all step through,
if we are ever to learn
that we are all One.

* * * * *

Rare earth

so, so ironic –
China drowning in toxicity,
red murderous
lakes of
mud;
workers inhaling death,
plants un-grown,

children un-birthed
for an energy-saving
light bulb for me.
Rare Earth –
I can hardly believe it.
It fills me with anger and
despair and
confusion.
Is there any way out?
any way to save this
oh-so-rare
Earth?
Energy-saving!
What are we talking about
here?
What do I know?
Why am I so ignorant?
Allowing others to talk
me into things,
allowing myself to not-know,
scoffing at those who don't
say what I say
believe what I believe?
Friends of the Earth!
If not now
When?!
In God's name –

And here is this
rare day –
so rare, it is the only
one of its kind –
never before and
never again.
It doesn't come more rare than that.
And this earth –
never before and
never again –
oh rare, rare Earth,
how precious you are
how endangered you are
with all your wealth and
beauty
all your gifts and potentials.
Is Gaia doomed?
And does that matter?
Yes –
No matter how far we go
to live
to build our substitute
homes and planets and
gardens
we would have failed in
our first marriage,
our first test
our first mother and friend
and lover.

I can't even think about what could be good from all the
learning
we might do,
because this treasure,
this rare and wonderful
Earth
would have been
abused to death.

Oh, the arrogance of ignorance.
Where is our humility,
our gratitude
in the face of this
priceless gift,
this rare Earth?

$$* * * * *$$

Riaño

All those villages
all that history
all those stories
all that rage and loss
the culture of centuries
the heart of this valley
(beneath these magnificent peaks)
battered, betrayed, drowned –
disappeared.
Not forgotten – yet –
(only 25 years ago – [and Franco signed the orders])

but once the heart is removed
what remains can only be
Life-like.

Silent bells – El Silencio de Campanes –
Other churches ring the hour
but nobody comes to pray
in holy shipwrecks.

death

God, I'm tired
and weary of
tiredness,
but it will go on.

~

So is that it? It should be –
Enough is enough
and it's already been too much.
Almost in a coma –
Eyelids flickered
as I squeezed her hand
and then withdrew my own;
Otherwise, just the ticking clock,
voices in the corridor,
and the wheeze of each short breath
(And the click of the 'driver'
as it delivered its comfort
intravenously)
Maybe not too long or too much
after all,
maybe just right.

(M died that night.)

~

And then I woke around 2.30
and my body was my mother's body
and it was M's
and my mother's was M's
and all were mine and not mine
moving towards death
becoming, being one body.

Iconography

An enormous, solitary marble 'portal' – 20' high and 12' wide – stands on the west coast of Naxos, near the port of Hora, or Naxos Town. The Portara was the entrance to a temple to Apollo that was never finished. Most of the original stone was removed over the centuries and reused, but some remaining blocks still lie scattered on the landward side of the 'Great Door'. The monumental 'frame' seems almost to float in space – an enigmatic threshold – through which the sky and the sea are offered in a riddling version of reality. For me, this monument is the embodiment of the icon-like nature of Greek landscapes and seascapes: in their elemental simplicity they draw one over a threshold between the worlds of Now and Then, or of this moment and deep time: the scales and measures we are accustomed to using shift and shake free.

Iconography

Panayia Krifti

800 careful steps down
sea, sky
silence

Sigri

And when it was over
silence –
everything destroyed
simplified
whole.

Olive Tree

rock-rooted
dry
time-corded
old

hard-stoned black fruit
golden oil

Icon 1

sea rock sky
olive pine
tamarisk
white blue
shade
sunset
night

Icon 2

ash grit sand
pebble
rock boulder
twist crush erode
transform

        * * * * *

He knew what he was saying when
he said
Wine dark sea.
Even though I doubt he'd seen any other;
But this – drunken, dark, everlastingly
part of all of us, blessed and cursed
and visited by the Gods, who flung
bits of landscape around as if
it was popcorn,
whose rages and couplings created
caves and mountains and streams and
valleys, labyrinths and monsters,
Gorgons and sea-creatures, nymphs and
naiads, beauty and terror, songs and
music,
revenge,
despair,
desolation,
disorientation,
madness and cunning.
Metamorphosis.

Grave Poetry – Delos (Museum translations)

A small carved stone showing a boy trying to bail out his boat; inscribed gravestones of drowned or shipwrecked individuals: the starkness of life for those who lived on the islands and traded on those treacherous and bountiful and beautiful waters transmitted itself in the words chosen in remembrance of lost children or friends. I copied four of these inscriptions down in my notebook, in the translations offered by the museum.

1.

Phokos died in a foreign land
His black vessel could not withstand the waves
and went down in the Aegean Sea.
It could not withstand the fury of the South Wind.
Now they have erected an empty monument for him
in his fatherland, and Promethis, his mother
everyday goes there lamenting like the bewailing bird
and saying how untimely death took her son.
(310 BC Phalaikos)

2.

Between Delos and Syros, Menoitis, Son of Diaphoneas
along with his cargo of Samian wine, was drowned.
He was in a hurry out of concern. But the sea does not spare:
even those who hasten to go to their sick father.
(1st Century BC Apollonidas)

3.

Hierokdis and his boat shared the same life.
They grew old together, and together they died.
He and Her – his faithful companion.
No other vessel ran more smoothly over the waves!
She was helping him until his old age. And finely
She became his grave: together they went down to Hades.
(1st Century BC Antiphilos)

4.

Cretans have always been unjust bandits and pirates!
Whoever of the Cretans knows what means justice?
They attacked me also, Timolytes,
travelling with a poor cargo.
The seabirds lament for my death.
But no grave covers Timolytes.
(3rd Century BC Leonidas from Taras)

And the sea and the sky, in all their changeableness, never
change.

Now sitting in Hora, Naxos, with people
from the Vodaphone 'whale' (with the huge
mouth) pouring out and all the jaws
of the studio and apartment Reps –
'Dimitra', 'Bourgos', 'Mike's',
'Windmill', 'Plaka', 'Adriana' –
stand ready to snap up anybody
who doesn't know where to go,
where to stay.
the feeding frenzy abates; Vodaphone
departs; but the Reps hang around
waiting for our ferry, the ferry to
Paros.

Nice breeze, comings and goings, farts
and splutters of motorbikes; bump
and rattle of wheeled baggage;
shouts in Greek, horns, backpacks,
gulls, fishing boats, sailing boats.

＊ ＊ ＊ ＊ ＊

A kingfisher skimmed over the water
this morning – yards from me – I
saw him coming – straight as
an arrow over the pastel pink
and blue water. He peeped a greeting

(I fancy) and continued onto the
rocks or into the tamarisk
below the Kastraki Taverna.
Lucky me.

* * * * *

Yesterday to Zeus' Cave where Dionysus,
the twice-born,
was birthed from Zeus' thigh,
full-term,
having been pulled from the dying
Semele
months before.
Goats – silky, bells sounding soft
and loud, croaks and gongs – what a
sound – around a hundred or more necks –
first down the long path on the
opposite side of the gorge, then slowly,
musically, up our side.
Disconcerted but unruffled by us.
The biggest the last – a huge
mythical creature, twice as big
as the biggest of the others – Pan.
He stood on his back legs, as high
as the shrub he grazed, and cast a
yellow eye on me as I passed.

* * * * *

If only I could remember:
every moment can be a new beginning –
not like going back to the beginning
and doing it again –
that's not possible –
but more like – sufficient unto the day –
and then there is the next day –
a journey – a day's trip –
what you can do in a day –
then let it go –

On the ferry to Samos –
beautiful thrumming
humming Spirit of Samos –
no, Samos Spirit –
slow boat to Samos – Thanks, God –
lots of time on the water –
time to say good-bye to Ikaria
as it passes into its own morning,
returns to its own stories,
its saints and winds and stars
its granites and holly oaks and
pines and planes and chestnuts and olives –
its well-fed cats and friendly dogs –
its Ikarian kilometres
and wines and pies and honey –
its waves and whales and eagles
slowly disappearing while we slide past
unknown and unexplored Fornoi,
as the huge mountain end of Samos

fills my view –
as a soldier sleeps on the lifejacket box
next to me – young and handsome –
as the Aegean goes on being,
carrying ferries and people and goods...
Ikaria becomes a misty silhouette –
yesterday's journey –

Oh, let go, Peggy, let go, and you lose nothing.

* * * * *

Three old dinghies
orange, yellow and blue –
blue and darker blue –
All in a line, offshore from
Stratos's place.
The water is perfectly still
and I swim soundlessly,
able to see the little black fish
and the silvery ones with a black stripe
below me.
The sun strikes my cheek –
hot off the water –
The yellow dinghy is beautiful,
on a yellow buoy –
its waterline and bottom –
once Greek blue on top of warm red;
now all colours together
glow warmly in the mirror of water on which it floats
like a poem.

Nea Roda

The tenderness:
disabled child under a beach brolly,
mother I judged too quickly,
attentive,
wasted arms of young man/boy
spasm in the air –
The sea rolls past –
our ouzo gets warm –
The large Mama Saint
– Aghia Mama –
puts suntan lotion on;
About 5 pm – after lunch –
by Paraskevi and Pantaleimon
at Aghios Nikolaos –

A gull flew over me in Nea Skori
this morning and I felt:
Precious Human Life.

Mama touches her son,
rolls his head back upright –
holds his shoulders
as his head lolls –
How amazing to see this.

The Ark

Every human body (including that
of the labourer, the fisherman, the shepherd
and the whore) is the ark
of the universe with its message.
(Nikiforos Vrettakos)

* * * * *

'I could live in a tent by the river,'
I think,
as I watch the man fishing from the bank,
throwing his line in
('casting' it – so much better a word)
over and over again –
the little pink bobbin plopping down
and being reeled in, willingly –
I think, 'I don't need or want a house.'
and I know I mean the confinement,
the too-much-indoors-ness
of a house –

The water here by Buccleugh Gardens
is soft – softly flowing, softly touched by the wind –
the boats and their reflections sit softly
and the trees have surrendered to the autumn,

still full of leaf, but their green-ness
draining inwards – back from the edges
that shone in the sun in the spring;
soft but alive – the water –
the depths hidden –
the moon pulling invisibly in the daylight,
but still pulling
(though gently, right now).
And the fisherman passes
and I think: he's my odd neighbour
(my odd ex-neighbour)
who I judged harshly
and who I now find myself
admiring, somewhat enviously –
the fisherman with a light step –
some sort of a God in disguise
(I think) – Pan, perhaps,
or some older-than-time Joker
or Fisher King
or Fisher of souls –

The gulls swoop
the little birds are now quiet
in the scrubby willow by the bank

The tide is on pause
the water barely moving – only the tiniest breath of wind
moves it
And now! 2 circles of ripples
where the fisherman threw (cast!) his line –

Now the fish rise to real insects –
laughing, I suspect –

My first fisherman-thought had been:
'I get it – fishing is not about catching a fish
(perhaps you even hope not to catch a fish)
and, back to Mencius or somebody –
the 'fish' you are after is the peace
of quiet emptiness –
the non-fish –
everything else is simply the fish-weir,
the 'apparatus' or 'vehicle' – or excuse! No,
it is more than that, much more,
requiring nothing less than everything.
It is a choice –
one loves and longs for something
so deeply
that everything else is released –
and that is a choice –
and the reward is worth it –
nothing is lost because a whole is gained.

Two cormorants!
Joy!
And I'm back to Lemnos
and my last morning swim
in the presence of a cormorant.

* * * * *

'These are the Gods,' I thought,
when I saw the limping deliverer of newspapers
(Where is his ancient dog?)
He seems to have spent all his lifetime of energy,
and now, solitary, pulls his paper-carrier
as if it were Sisyphus's rock.

then I saw the rough-sleeper
young but worn
keeping going, probably known to all,
but always alone.
These are the Gods –
walking amongst us,
invisible, apparently wretched...

                    * * * * *

What I'm thinking about is what the
options are
when you see no more need for God, or
when you see through god.
What do you see?
Is it blue sky? and is that sacred, or is
it just the atmosphere composed of bits
of chemicals and light? and is
that then sacred and the Mystery?
Where is the mystery? is there none?
I was thinking about vision quests
and what happens to messages and
images that come to us – that don't

feel as if they come from us –
Are they just weird bits of the brain
that can be located and have
names, or does that locate the mystery
in the brain; does that call the
mystery 'amygdala' instead of God?
Does that make the brain sacred?
So what about dawn or dusk or birth
or death or sunlight or the ocean or
courage or the Milky Way? Maybe they
just are and some of us feel the mystery
shining in them and through them and so
the mystery is us
and our capacity for –
our permeability to –
light
our openness to other voices –
I think the 'American Indians'
(my stereotype of the American Indians)
sought to earth the light,
turn the lightning to
wisdom, sought to make the It
Thou,
so that it could be incorporated
into the world of choice and action
rather than dismissed or questioned, as to
its reality.
It was accepted and thought about,
de-mystified but honoured.

* * * * *

We knew we were small,
weak in comparison with the great beasts
and the blasts of heat and cold
which came from the sky
and the earth;
but we gained some of their bigness
by song and prayer, by watching and remembering
by painting and singing and dancing their strength
by taking upon us their furs and feathers –
antlers –
by eating them –
and because we recognized and honoured their life force
their spirit,
they gave it to us willingly,
having recognized a similar heart and courage
and beauty –

What do we have now,
which tells us these things,
against which we measure ourselves,
not in order to conquer
but in order to worship
to recognize and be
recognized by?

So, my thoughts continued –
What do we measure ourselves against?
And I thought – only Death – and then I thought –

Against how successful we are in conquering Death –
and disease –
and later I thought – is that so very different?
And then I thought...
I think so,
but I haven't worked it out yet.

* * * * *

Buddha

tidy little female Labrador
manoeuvring a huge 'stick'
(a 4' branch)
in and around and under a stile
while her patient and trusting
owner holds the gate open –
Buddha:
knowing we have to do it,
all by ourselves,
but never withholding help
or encouragement –
holding the gate open even
as we fix our eyes on the big stick.
"No problem baffles great zeal"
because there is tender help
around, unseen, unacknowledged
probably, when we finally succeed
(or not)

Time and Tide

(From my notes on the day)

I stopped to watch the eddies and flow of the river and felt
eased by its beautiful, changing surface and the weed that was
visible in its shallow waters, anchored and streaming in the
flow. I wondered what caused the little eddies and whirlpools:
a feature on the bottom or something which had fallen in from
above, causing a disturbance? I recalled doing the gesso for
the Enso and hoping that a flaw in the rabbit-skin glue-soaked
hessian would become invisible under 17 layers of gesso. No.
Every layer simply reproduced it. I should have known – and
probably did. But, I think now, that and my other 'mistakes'
resulted in a cosmic Enso of unexpected and chaotic beauty
and order. Turbulence. Instead of the perfectly burnished gold
Enso on a flawlessly smooth gold leaf base, which I had
envisioned, I ended up with a great swirling icon of movement
and life.

...And then I recognized the obvious: the sky and air were
charged with stormy energy, even if it didn't do its spectacular
[forecasted] bit it was a huge weather system and it was
affecting the skies above me and the 'weather' inside me. The
continuing notion that the elemental world is somehow
outside us and we are separate from it, regardless of
barometric pressure or the amount of electrical energy in the
atmosphere is clearly a delusion. Once I had said to myself, 'Of
course I'm feeling all over the place and not knowing where or

how I want to be, feeling uneasy, disordered, not quite in my skin. Just look at the skies and feel the atmosphere.' I felt better. Two dogs – on separate occasions – ran into the road and were nearly killed by cars; my horrible coffee was overflowing the cup when it was handed to me, lurching from side to side – the saucer awash. I have to see how I get shaped by the 'turbulences' of my life, shaped by what is deep in me – my bedrock or river bed – by what drops in unexpectedly 'from above' and gets carried along on the surface, or drops into the deeper flow, shaped by what is growing within, anchored or flowing, shaped by the 'weather'.

* * * * *

Seasons

The wind hurls blue sky and havoc
at trees released by rain, thirst-quenched, drunken,
bending and bucking – tidal sweep and shush,
rising and falling.
And now all is wind.
Rumpled ducks hunch up into the lee shore,
as streaking cats' paws fly across the ponds.
Dogs tangle their leads; children disobey –
unleashed, unanchored, deafened by the sound.
Trees strain against their roots to wrench them free,
While darkening clouds break, scatter, join and fly.
Wind whips my hair into my eyes and makes
my coat into a spinnaker of blue;
And I too am unleashed yet tangled, dark
and glancing, dangerous and changeable.

Wind roaring the washed-blueness
of the sky through trees
madly in love with their freedom,
that bend and dance and rear back –
(though some try to hush its wildness)
Birch seeds fly in the windows.

What if trunks and roots
released their leafy parachutes
and, with my spinnaker coat,
sent all of us flying
sky high?
Let's go!

Now blue sky is black
and joy turns to menace.
What living thing would not fear this force –
feel its pulse race
as the trees strain against their roots?

        * * * * *

I have a photo of [my 4-year old daughter]
asleep in the sun in the sleeping bag that went everywhere
with her
– lightweight and lime green –
It's summer, getting on for 50 years ago,
and it's the Okanagan.
Her body is soft and hot,
at one with the heat and sleep,

utterly surrendered to both.
You wouldn't need to know that it was summer, in the
Okanagan,
to know it was hot:
her round, soft arm and flushed soft face would tell you.

Today, just now, on a day of still heat and full sun,
I approached the area in Kew
where the tall cedars and redwoods and cypresses are
gathered,
and I greeted them, wondering how they were holding up
in the heat.
I saw the same surrender, the same soft weight
of non-resistance
of saturated heat.
And I gently compared that to my almost-fear of too-hot
(or too-cold, or too-windy, or too-tired, or too-old)
And I knew there was an equally gentle message here,
and I remembered the photo.

       * * * * *

Overwhelmed by the beauty of this
autumn day, its fresh breeze, its
mystery. Is it a conclusion, or a
turning inwards, the beginning
of the stillness that will be winter –
the trees seem to belong more to themselves –
the birds reclaim their
wings, their bird-ness.

All around me a soft yellowing is
happening – dropping from the late
afternoon sky into the trees, which
hold it, like jewels of unseen moisture.
The water of the Ponds is a liquid
reflection of the bending, browning
grasses that love this wind, love
to bend to it, towards the sun.

* * * * *

Time – the ending or middle or
beginning of a season –
this morning, before the earliest
part of the day cleared into
brilliant blue sky
and warmth, passing a beech tree,
the phit and splatter and plunk
stopped me in my
tracks.
Parakeets? No. Pigeons!? No.
Squirrels – busy hands and teeth
grasping, nibbling, tossing away –
I sat on a bench below and heard
the thuck and scatter and ricochet of
shell and nibbled seed
all around me on the ground lay
the remains of earlier feasts –
nuts half-nibbled,
shells green and brown, smooth

inside, hairy-hard without.
A sound to my left:
an upside-down squirrel
unceremoniously scrabbling for
the ripest nuts, low down, way
out on the branch.
Don't stand on ceremony!
Feast! Waste! Enjoy!
The season of beech nuts is
glorious, mad, a harbinger
of autumn, a spray of
ecstatic beauty and abundance.

* * * * *

This place, this moment, is perfect and fleeting –
new and old –
the wind moves the trees
the acorns fall.

There's a madness in the stags
and in the squirrels:
now – mine – quick – life – death.

* * * * *

It's the urgency of autumn which is so hard, so pressing –
All the un-done bits become a minefield –
The end approaches and I'm not ready
More alarmingly,
will there be time to change everything, to

do it better
before time runs out?
Maybe not.

* * * * *

creamy fallow deer buck bucking into the bracken,
head lowered – charge and thrust – head up –
Actaeon
defiant
another charge and thrust –
we stare at each other
and I feel like stamping my foot at him

* * * * *

Surf

At the centre of it – the
sound that comes from the breaking
open of the centre, a living
centre. A roar.

They say there is a roar which
accompanies an earthquake,
and, I think, also an eruption.
I think it's the same – the
living heart of the thing
roars as it explodes into
a new form.
Do we do that?

* * * * *

Seaweed

Sleek and feathery, knobbed and
lobed like some ocean heart
or lungs,
corrugated, shining – in
heaps and strewn for acres
over the beach where families with buckets and windbreaks
surfers
and children in wetsuits
pick their way.
55 seagulls also pick –
a feast for the famished –
they scream at each other as
discoveries are made,
morsels fought over,
a starfish, a crab, an
opened mussel, wrenched
from its hold.

Brown and red and green and yellow,
tossed by the tide
blown and billowed
by the underwater currents.
Live, still alive, with the
rhythms of the ocean,
painted into forms now lying
beached, heaped and tangled.

Almost inconceivable:
the unwithstandable force –
dissatisfied until it had dislodged
every root and tentacle,
every hairy hand-hold –
pulled and yanked
wrenched and tore, and finally,
having achieved its aim,
chucked
this brown and gleaming carpet
at our feet

* * * * *

I like to subtract
human beings and human things
from a view
or a landscape or a seascape
(as in this case, as I watch the surf
breaking, breaking against
Pentire Point),
to go back to deep time
which is almost timelessness
and imagine those waves
breaking through eons of time
against the land;
cliff, rock, sand
being slowly, slowly eroded
or uplifted by the momentous
grinding – oh, so slow – of plates of rock

formed from upwellings
from deep, deep below the seas
moving soundlessly
pushing and twisting and fracturing
pressing and crushing
the earth making itself
over and over again
and the sea breaking and breaking
against it

And then maybe I imagine
as I did about an hour ago,
birds,
only birds, in the air
and the sea breaks
and they cry to each other
over the sound of the waves
   and nobody is there
   to hear them
sounds – sea and seabirds
And of course, I am there
   even though I am not
but I'm hearing the sounds
   no voices, no cars
   no human things
   that make noise

And the low September sun
glows golden on rolling white surf;
but there is no September,

only a turning and a turning,
a breaking and a breaking
and a making
and the gulls' cries
and the roar of the surf.

I thought: no matter what the land was
(forest, mountain, cliff)
the sea was always just the sea
moved by the moon
by the turning of the moon
by the turning of the earth
and its forces and elements
currents and tides and winds

always there
throughout deep, deep
timeless
time

And now I've stripped that
smooth green cover
and soft, containing earth
away,
and it's bare rock
Galapagos rock,
sharp and young
even here
and still the sea
just breaks and breaks.

* * * * *

the wave story:
waves (and human lives):
processes, not things,
moving energy fields
full of living power and potential;
in which there are exchanges of energy
and transformations of energy;
and there are capillary
waves and gravity waves
and then there are deep-rolling
swells and currents

shaped by the sea floor and the earth's deep processes
of creating and destroying.

And the moment
the wave reaches land and breaks
is the moment which gives
closure to the story of that
wave, so that it no longer
is the plaything of wind
and tide and earth's deep shifts.
The beauty – the
majesty of the wave as it breaks and dies
is not very different to our own deaths –
the rounding surge, the transfer
of energy, the release –
and the beautiful shush or
airborne spray (gulls wheeling through it)
or whisper of a ripple that arrives,
at last, on a distant shore
(and is home)

* * * * *

Fluctuations are waves –
improbable, infinitely variable
sparking matter
and anti-matter
in an instant so brief, it almost isn't –
and then they aren't –

except, except
there's that thing, that tiny improbable thing,
which isn't going to buy
the simple cancellation of plus and minus,
that thing that keeps it all going,
improbably,
keeps it becoming,
rather than stopping
for once and for all.
I could call it Life,
this beautiful imbalance,
this exquisite improbability.

* * * * *

I see that all things are continuously being born
dying, colliding, slipping past each other,
touching, melting...
everything in the process of becoming –
itself –
or something else...
patterns emerge and build,
and drop away,
bend and weave – moving, moving –
Like the screen-saver on my laptop.

* * * * *

Fullness of time,
that's the phrase –
the fullness of time, when it spills over,
when it completes itself
or when something – in its completion –
is born,
or, perhaps, dies.

* * * * *

Everything that is
some-thing vanishes –
Vast and beautiful Emptiness
exploding into Being
flashing into Eternity.
No wonder I didn't get it:
I was thinking so small,
or so concretely.

Healing

Ring the bells that still can ring;
Forget your perfect offering;
There's a crack in everything;
It's how the light gets in.
(Leonard Cohen[4])

Healing

(1)

I become a vegetable thing
a body thing
little more
My face turns to the Sun
life-giver
bone-mender
No thought
Just breathing bones
and skin

(2)

Hammamelis
Witch Hazel
Bitter-sweet blossoms of mid-winter
seeking the sun
A robin shows me there is food
(when I thought he was seeking a hand-out):
tiny yellow seeds
Mahonia?
Witch Hazel?
A Blackbird spreads his tail
and does a jump – at me!
Does he want me to piss off?
Is my warm spot in this small, sheltered temple
his?
And only comparatively warm,

on this mid-winter day;
The Witch Hazel glows –
Each lemon-yellow tendril-y finger
curled to catch and hold
and breathe in
the cold-warm winter day.

(3)

Easter Monday
After and before –
the moment in-between –
I pause on a bench
on my way for a coffee.
Spring has leapt out of the ground
(a woodpecker loudly announces
his ability to make an impressive hole)
with the bit of sun from yesterday,
and now it is joyously proclaiming
its dominance
blue sky, chestnut buds
birds on every bush and tree –
short-sleeved visitors
warm sun – full brightness –
Me in duvet coat, but with sunhat
tucked in my bag.
Let this period go now,
release it –
recovery is frightening
brings choices

(brings the need to <u>make</u> choices)
to believe in the potential of
the inner disorder that
needs to be freed to form and reform
throughout the whole
next cycle.
Out of the duvet coat, gloves, hat
more uncovered
fewer places to hide
or take cover
or be pardoned
(or pardon myself)
It's been a long season of realignment
(8 months and counting)
– not really undertaken voluntarily –
now I think maybe my compassion
has been reset or recalibrated
and I must needs 'go
where I have to go' – or,
at least,
rejoin my journey in good heart.
Thanks.

(4)

The other world, from which butterflies and buzzards and
blackbird feathers
and magpie feathers
appear, to console us /
and console us,

what and where is this world?
My heart tells me it is the place of the heart
where the heart reaches, stretches, yearns,
maybe almost utters a name
and is met
in the heart's language
(that's the really important part)
The language is one of prayer and response
opening out and receiving
'The Second bush and I are one,'
(I wrote)
but that was after years of opening and waiting
and then suddenly, it wasn't there.
I can't explain that
Maybe it's as if it was a door,
that had opened
rather than a wall –
the visibility of the bush / wall
became
luminously absent
and there was just the deer
his spirit
and he/she walks to me – right now
gently, delicately

There is a clearing,
a sacred space.
Thanks.

Return

'*When Lao-tzu* (the 'author' of the *Tao Te Ching*) *says, "All are clear, I alone am clouded," he is expressing what I now feel in advanced old age. Lao-tzu is the example of a man with superior insight who has seen and experienced worth and worthlessness, and who at the end of his life desires to return into his own being, into the eternal unknowable meaning... This is old age and a limitation. Yet there is so much that fills me: plants, animals, clouds, day and night, and the eternal in man. The more uncertain I have felt about myself, the more there has grown up in me a feeling of kinship with all things. In fact it seems to me as if that alienation which so long separated me from the world has become transferred into my own inner world, and has revealed to me an unexpected unfamiliarity with myself.' (C. G. Jung[5])*

---

[5]   Jung, C. G., p. 98

Return

Part I: Doing only what is necessary / Acting from a quiet place
1.

Do only what needs to be done –
then it is an extension
of the being of the Moment
(still at-One)
do more and something is created
which will have an opposite
To return to the Undivided
the Unconditioned
is Rest – The Whole –

2.

Do only what is necessary –
It's a bit like sitting on a[n exercise] ball:
big movements tend to lead to
more big – corrective – movements;
small, even tiny, adjustments
work better,
keep you closer to where things
are steadily in balance –
dynamically in balance –
And it's okay to start now
(having not started a long time ago)

I don't have to go back over everything;
there's nothing to be done about it,
and I did the best I was able to do.

Then (now) release it (it's gone, anyway)
and try something a bit different.

3.

Do only what's necessary
Say only what's necessary
(Beyond that you bring something into the world
into existence.)
Rising naturally, it will also fall, naturally
(if I don't bring something else up
which adds energy to it)
Let it go.

4.

I've learned a lot
about
only what is necessary
(no more)
and it may be that what is necessary
is huge
and requires all of one's strength
to restrain or release
to stay still
or find stillness

of heart and mind –
quiet, when disquieted –

I'm learning

How do I know what is necessary?
Maybe first, I must return
to the root
to rest
to the Undivided
(and become, myself, undivided,
cool
quiet)
then, I think, what is necessary
can become clear
and maybe it's nothing
other than the necessity
of stillness

So few words are necessary
ever
'Perhaps', or 'Ah!', or, 'I see'
maybe they will do for most things

Part II: *The Rainmaker* (in my words)

A certain area in China had not had any rain for a very long period and the drought had finally become so severe that the villagers decided to invite a Rainmaker to come and see if he could rectify the situation. A message was sent and he duly arrived. He chose to stay in a small hut on the edge of the village. He took his few possessions there and the wait began. He was seen to go out early with his wheelbarrow to fetch wood from the woodcutter, and a bit later, with his bucket, to draw water from the well. He swept the small area in front of the entry to the hut, and otherwise nobody saw him or heard anything. During the day smoke came out of the little pipe in the roof, and at night it was dark and quiet. On the 7th day it rained. The villagers came to thank the Rainmaker and to ask him what he had done. He told them all he had done was that which was necessary to his simple existence, nothing more: to fetch wood and water when needed, to rest when it was dark, and to care for the little hut. By returning to the roots of life, he created (or recreated), the balance that had been lost.

'Yet...'
Such a small word
lying within a breath,
almost a sigh,
barely a sound...
some movement within
– a turning –
releases (but doesn't discard
or discredit)
one version
and allows
(gently – not insistently)
another possibility

A feather is balanced
against the heavy weariness
of having seen so much
(too much)
of life and the world,
the limitations of mortality, balanced
by a cloud
day and night
'and the eternal in man'

Kaleidoscope

Cafe Hollyhock – lovely!
Snow falling, kids screaming
in delight,
sledges bumping and clattering
over icy, muddy, snowy bumps –
(the robin is uninterested in
black sunflower seeds)
Cinnamon box for T and F –
So, is what I am doing
the miso soup exercise?
...the robin and
the black sunflower seeds and the
cinnamon box
and my tea and
the smell of snow
and the remembrance of other
joyous, brief snowy times...
am I painting the One
in the Many – trying to –
no, simply rejoicing in
the possibility of
remembering NOW
in its totality, through
the jogging of sense memory
of the particular bits.

The flakes are big and soft and slow –
colour is fading and people become
Lowry silhouettes
Currier and Ives folk.

Is this what we want
from cameras – this sort of
re-creation, jogging of our recall?

I don't know
and it doesn't matter.

The robin is back
maybe trying my seeds again
to see if he was too hasty,
mistaken.

The arms of the old plane tree
are caught in mid-swing,
a winter Snow dance.

My tea runs out
the flakes fall –
a Japanese moment of
silence and movement,
Earth, Heaven, Man –
and a madly skittering squirrel
completes the scene!

(later)
How can I explain? (I thought)
I've seen a lot of winters, I guess –
this is my 69th –
and they are...
I don't know.
Now I am left with a sense of
wonder at the beauty I've just
seen, walked in –
the snow as a blessing
which falls in beauty. I wanted to say,
'You see,'
(I can imagine)
'a grey-haired lady with
a black duvet coat on,
walking with care,
carrying a "Petersham Nurseries"
bag, not a sledge,
and I look old or
different to you
and I am – because I am aware
of this moment and my feelings
about it and its beauty –
I am seeing myself, and you;
seeing this winter scene and
remembering previous ones –
when my kids were the squealers;
and then I saw your Mums
as my Mum,

and me as the small, excited one;
then I saw my grandson the
other day, red-cheeked and
screaming for joy and my son –
the adult, now.'

Time slips like a kaleidoscope
into different patterns –
same coloured pieces:
snow, child, adult, and
cautious grey-haired lady –
turn the tube and they all shift.
'Inside', I wanted to say,
'I am not this cautious lady,
so easily dismissed,

104

(so recognizable and so unknown)
I am ageless – without age –
unknowable.'
Well, I thought, they can't know
nobody can know
until or
unless or
ever. And then there was the snow
and the Park
and I never wanted to go in –
and the Second Bush is Life,
and I will sit in front of it
happily
all my days
and let it reveal itself to me
millimetre by millimetre,
one snowflake at a time,
one leaf at a time,
and be so full of gratitude
that my heart grows
huge.

* * * * *

So long ago I stood
among the trees
and felt the world around me
(the sound world)

to be like a piece of raw linen,
each small irregularity
(which made it beautiful)
being like the little (or big)
sounds I was hearing
– but the fabric was One –
one thing –
not broken or spoiled
or finite:
behind the sound of a voice
or a bird, or a scrabbling squirrel,
or a car, or a plane,
(heard for an instant
and then no more),
the fabric of silence and space
stretched forever –
and it was all one.
And now I'm with this again –
But now it can be
a thought (in my mind)
or a sensation (in my body)
a sudden fear or queasiness
and they too can be experienced
in that way,
I discover –
heard or felt,
unsettling, intrusive,
they're also just little
marks of raw life

in the fabric of space –
vast emptiness

And – of course – the fabric
isn't outside of me;
it's the vastness of inside,
the 'fabric' of boundaryless
mind.

Finally, one of those moments when the sheer number of
years that have passed in one's life between a remembered
event and its reminder in the present – its echo – is
recognized with a sense of shock.

To sit still
with unease
and queasiness,
emptiness
gnawing at the edges
of the flake of presence
that remains

is not easy

Even when the sun is shining
on a glorious September afternoon
and the river
is a blue drift
behind the trees
and the sun is warm on my face
and the birds are singing

a gentle happy song

The beautiful Mummy
and her baby, bound closely,
and her toddler
(for whom everything has gone wrong)
wend their way up the path
of the Terrace Gardens –

and 48 years have passed
since I first came here.

P.S.

Once upon a time
as I walked in a nearby wood
something inexplicable happened
and a voice said
Know this for what it is

Book II

Part 1

'...And what you thought you came for
Is only a shell, a husk of meaning
From which the purpose breaks only when it is fulfilled
If at all. Either you had no purpose
Or the purpose is beyond the end you figured
And is altered in fulfilment...'[6]

Eliot's lines from *Little Gidding* reflect a continuing experience for me: Over the years of noting and writing, I was unaware of any purpose other than to join myself and the moment and the place where I found myself as openly and honestly as possible. That was all I 'came for'. At some point that 'shell' opened and, years after I had started, and in the wake of events and passing time, I 'purposefully' decided to look back over what I had written, with no particular end in view, until a further 'end' did come into view: to gather some of my writings into a small book aimed at others who might, like me, be reflecting on age, on the place where they found themselves in their own journey. This then required an effort to introduce the themes I had visited over the years, to look at my writings more objectively, to consider what I thought I wanted to offer to a reader, some other individual beside myself. I had a 'goal' – not the same thing as a purpose, but not unrelated.

---

[6]   Eliot, T. S., p. 215

Having gathered and introduced the material, moving ever deeper into it, a friend suggested I should offer a sort of 'road map'. I attempted to do this, but such a map eluded me, and the effort to organize the work in this way seemed to deaden and reduce it, to shape it into something which had a false or contrived structure or purpose. (If the age-old instruction is to look not at the finger pointing to the moon but beyond it, to the moon itself, then I felt that seeking to produce a road map left me looking harder at the finger hoping to find the moon there.) I had to recognize that the structure of the book was almost incidental; it did not reveal any conscious, overarching message; the individual writings 'mapped' moments of being, in different moods and landscapes, inner and outer, and that was that.

I abandoned the entire project, having no sense at all of where I was heading with it. It is not entirely true to say I abandoned it: it was more that I abandoned the idea that I could wrestle the material into some form by naming what I knew, by describing the surface, the 'husk of meaning'. In fact, I knew I had come to a dead end in terms of conscious manipulation and that I needed to wait on the material itself to call me back, recall me.

Rough Edges

'Rough Edges' is an attempt to introduce the original writings. They are not poems; they are not prose; they are records of moments in which an unusual quality of immediacy and intimacy was experienced – created and discovered through an intentional participation – with the moment – that was both passive/receptive and active/constructive. Holding both the with-out and the with-in, as best I could was a bit like tasting something and then while the taste is on your tongue, tentatively seeking words that convey that taste, that quality: tasting and staying with the taste – staying present to the taste.

As I started to look back over my notebooks, it was fairly clear which writings I would like to include and which to leave out. This sifting continued over the months, much as the contents of the pocket were continually re-evaluated. Also, while it felt important to not try to tidy them up or to make them into anything other than what they were, nonetheless, I had to work hard to accept their 'rough edges', the too-frequent repetition of particular words or phrases, the questionable punctuation, the confusion, the drama, the hyperbole of some lines. I recognized later that the dashes which appear at the end of so many lines represent moments – short or long – when I paused, not knowing what, if anything, would follow. The dash completed – while leaving open to continuation – the preceding line and offered containment for the moment[s] of no-thought. Thus, it was a visual record of, or testimony to, an empty space of time, a waiting-to-see pause, an inner listening. Recognizing this, I decided to leave the vast majority of dashes/hyphens in, as irritating as they might be! The same goes for other punctuation marks, which might seem puzzling, and again, the same goes for phrases which feel 'rough' or overblown. I felt I was more comfortable with deselecting a whole piece than I was with trying to make it acceptable to a more critical Me.

Part 2

Time passed. In the back of my mind I was aware of a sort of web of connections between much that I had felt and written and read, but whenever I tried to focus on it the links went fuzzy and felt both much too complex and much too tenuous. Eventually, the powerful and moving effect of experiences that I had recorded in my notebooks reasserted themselves, urging me, yet again, to try to understand them better. And even if understanding didn't come, it felt as if carrying on was the only option I could trust that felt meaningful and authentic. This turning back – looping back over familiar ground – looking for what I might have missed originally, has its own inexhaustible and interminable dynamic, and, whether you fight it or submit to it, it promises nothing: perhaps, after all, there is no purpose to it. Yet, the drive persisted. Martin Buber wrote: '...a man goes his way and simply wishes that it might be *the* [my italics] way: in the strength of his wish, his striving is expressed. Waiting, not seeking, he goes his way.'[7]

---

[7] Buber, Martin, p.56

Benches

Over many years I have sought out benches in order to stop, to rest, to sketch, or, more than anything else, to make brief notes about where I have found myself, in the broadest sense of that phrase. About twenty years ago I began to use these moments in the day to explore this terrain more sensitively or with more patience, more openness; and thus, over time, benches grew to represent more than just a place to stop: they became in themselves an extraordinary, unconditional space whose qualities of stillness and silence were inexhaustible, a space in which I felt safe enough to 'drop my guard', to release my self-consciousness, to *lose myself*. Like the Tao, they just *were*.

Although characterized by different levels of comfort, different views, they were where this book started.

Part 3

Thinking about those months of 're-viewing' the journey, I picture a path or a highway littered with bits of trash and debris – rejected ideas, misapprehended purposes: I go back to gather up the unsightly mess, pick up a piece of paper, reread it, think, 'Oh, I see now what I was trying to say,' or 'I see I got only so far with this because it had a built-in limitation – a piece missing from that jigsaw right from the start,' or, 'But that links up with that other thought I had; why didn't I see that?' Recognizing this was interesting; it made me more aware of an energy or process that had been carrying me for a long time. It was as if I was watching an old black and white film being rerun in which I was walking along a road, getting older, having this experience or that, my face lighting up from time to time, making of it all that I could, occasionally apparently moving faster, then, maddeningly, retracing my footsteps, or stopping altogether. It helped me appreciate the length of this journey. But I wanted to shout, 'Hurry up! Time is running out...!' Now I see what has gone before and what continues to happen as a continuous journey, even if it has been one of looping back over and over again. Like a Mobius strip which flips itself into the symbol of eternity when you trace one side of it and find yourself on the other side, but know that both sides are one: it's the nature of the thing.

Moments

1.

When I sit by Richmond Bridge (or elsewhere, but particularly there) and feel I want to write, it is, in part, wanting to try to capture the moment, but not only that: perhaps it is more a sort of joyful demonstration to myself and to the Universe that I could write or list forever the elements of this moment and I would never, ever exhaust it, quite apart from the fact that it has already become the next 'this moment'. It can be felt as a whole – an indescribable whole, an undivided whole, a contingent whole, a compound of many other wholes – a bird dips towards the water – an infinity in that image – inexhaustible. But as I catalogue, knowing is an infinite catalogue, new and lively things keep catching my eye, all parts of this moment – somebody's shoe laces, a patient dog, that leaf, that wave – and it is joyous because it is inexhaustible and because it doesn't matter that it's inexhaustible. And I am a part of this great contingent arising – so fleeting, so beautiful.

Every moment has this at its centre: Me, Here, That – all interpenetrating.

2.

'Miso Soup' moments are light-hearted, celebratory: noticing details and then letting them go, more or less uninterrupted in their flight through the day. When I consider 'moments' in a wider sense, what they actually are – if they are anything –

and how or why I feel part of any given moment and not of another, it's more complicated.

An extended series of experiences that took place over a day or two illustrates something of what I had been trying to explore and understand for myself for such a long time, and also something of the process of wrestling with my experiences, trying to grasp the essential quality of these 'moments'.

I realize now that what I was unable to see was my own presence, present to the presence of trees and shadows and wind and water and scent and light.

3.

We remember where we were and what we were doing at the moment something momentous happens. It gets through to us; it wakes us up. Often it feels as if it comes 'out of the blue'. I think it is the felt experience of that moment of 'waking up' or being 'blown open' (see *Postscript*, below) that gives the moment its memorability even more than the content of the moment, which only anchors it in time or contextualizes it. There is a shock of some sort and we are off-balance, unprepared; we feel alive, present, for that moment, more aware of place and self and of that moment and of being at one with that moment, a moment we wouldn't have even noticed if nothing had 'happened'. And what has 'actually' happened – whether an assassination or an evening sunset – whatever – something unexpected – might be registered in one way in our memory, but I think it is the heart that is really blown open, touched. We are unlikely to get this effect if we try to capture or recapture or relate the event to somebody else, although we can remind ourselves of it and of the effect of feeling astonished, ambushed by something, alive, by retelling the 'story', by taking a photograph. Retelling or looking at a photo are prompts and also ways of trying to stay in contact with that thing that happened, because we don't want to lose it, that feeling. The photo may recall us to the moment when we were opened, moved – that is what we want: not the flower or the scene itself, but the effect the flower or the scene had on us.

The poem I admire and love probably more than any other is *Postscript*, by Seamus Heaney. The postscript is the bit we add at the end of a letter or message – its apparent 'afterthought-ness' belying the choice to put it there for maximum effect. It catches us off-guard, as it is intended to do, having a sideways sort of relationship to that which precedes it. We are left with it in a way that we are not with the main body of the letter which has been signed off by a goodbye of some sort and then a name or signature: all wrapped up and forgettable. The PS opens us up again; it is the carrier of a different 'voice', a different message, to which different rules apply: it's somehow what we really wanted to say all along. It has a different quality: it's the 'parting shot', delivered hand-on-the-doorknob, just before an exit. It might leave us feeling, *'What was that?'*

From the title to the final line, Heaney sets about to gently destabilize us, to unbalance the balances we continually seek to re-establish. Like the 'wind and the light', everything works off everything else and keeps the whole experience one of shifting attention as – softly and sideways – he 'buffets' us with vivid detail after vivid detail. And without fanfare he accomplishes exactly what he tells us it is 'useless' to attempt: he 'captures' a fleeting moment by joining it – lightly and lovingly – becoming a part of it for just long enough to pass it on to us. And then, as if the wind had finally succeeded in blowing open the door of the car we sit in, unprepared and off-guard, we, our hearts, are blown open.

Postscript

And some time make the time to drive out west
Into County Clare, along the Flaggy Shore,
In September or October, when the wind
And the light are working off each other
So that the ocean on one side is wild
With foam and glitter, and inland among the stones
The surface of a slate-grey lake is lit
By the earthed lightning of a flock of swans
Their feathers roughed and ruffling, white on white,
Their fully grown headstrong-looking heads
Tucked or cresting or busy underwater.
Useless to think you'll park and capture it
More thoroughly. You are neither here nor there,
A hurry through which known and strange things pass
As big soft buffetings come at the car sideways
And catch the heart off guard and blow it open.[8]

---

[8] Heaney, Seamus, p.70

Part 4

When streams and smaller rivers join the flow of a larger river, the whole nature of the 'body' of water changes. Similarly, discovering the words and ideas of others who had long ago mapped the territory I was exploring altered my 'flow', sometimes overwhelming me, other times leaving me feeling astonished and simply grateful. At a time when all my reviewing and gathering of scraps had begun to feel fruitless – yet again – a small, unobtrusive book caught my eye, and it did so probably because it contained the words, 'Wabi Sabi' in the title, although this time, Wabi Sabi referred not to an animal (see 'Healing'), but to a principle, or a force, a sort of energy, or a process. In *Wabi Sabi for Artists, Designers, Poets & Philosophers*, the author, Leonard Koren writes, '...beauty is a dynamic event that occurs between you and something else. Beauty is thus an altered state of consciousness, an extraordinary moment of poetry and grace.'[9] These two sentences were incredibly powerful for me: not only did they completely 'fit' my experiences – the experiences I had recorded in notebook after notebook – they also placed those moments into a far broader or more transformational field, within the vast concept of Beauty, Beauty not as a principle or as an inherent quality, but as an 'event' taking place in a moment. Koren's, 'poetry and grace' captured the lively – even radiant – dynamism and numinosity of the moments as I had experienced them. Furthermore, he had equated beauty with

---

[9]   Koren, Leonard, p.51

'an altered state of consciousness' and hadn't even tried to go beyond that definition, whereas I had struggled and failed to describe my state of consciousness. He said all that needed to be said – and perhaps all that could be said – in those twenty-seven words, and they were a huge gift to me. In fact, I would say, everything else followed on from them.

Words

1.

Wittgenstein warns us off pursuing speech beyond the reach of words. ('Whereof one cannot speak, thereof one must be silent.') It is easy to understand and accept this statement, but I think it is rather that we come to a boundary marking what can be expressed in ordinary speech, in language where agreed meanings of words – within a particular range – can be taken for granted. Beyond that fairly broad and fluid boundary we can either give up on communicating or seek other ways of conveying our intuitions, apprehensions, and feelings. Music, art and poetry have the capacity to express and communicate on another level, to touch us or evoke something in us which bypasses – or is not received so much by – the brain as by some other organ of awareness. The receptivity of this organ depends on its openness, its capacity to be moved (not necessarily emotionally), more like water that can allow the wave form to flow through it. Spaciousness or fluidity is necessary because the more dense or 'full' this medium already is, the less responsive is it possible for it to be. All forms of art, but perhaps music, in particular, have the advantage of being predominantly non-verbal by their nature. Music primarily engages the ear and is, therefore, uncomplicated by information from the other senses which can 'thicken' the medium.

Poetry relies on words, which, like music, are sounds, but to a much greater extent than ordinary speech, it depends, for its ability to 'move' us, on rhythm, pace, space. It evokes rather than describes, attracts something beyond the words into a relationship with the words. Wittgenstein's statement (in the English translation, as in the original) is poetic: he has succeeded in evoking the 'whereof', which is indescribable, not by attempting to describe it, but by repeating, and almost-repeating, words that are very 'open' within a rhythmic phrase that rises simply and then simply falls away.

In the Chinese Taoist classic, *The Tao Te Ching*, the words and phrases of the text are deliberately, if subtly, undermined by the inclusion of characters which suggest indefiniteness, or the fundamental inexpressibility of what is 'behind' the images, ideas, or thoughts which sit on the page. Words like, 'dim', or 'vague', or 'diffuse', or 'deep', or 'distant' convey this ineffable quality and 'thin out' the tendency to cling to the text. They suggest a reaching out for something – a meaning, or an understanding – which is important but tenuous and which lies beyond or beneath or between the words. They communicate a message along the lines that the reader or receiver of the message should also reach out, seek the subtle not the definite. I really like these soft reminders of the insubstantiality of words and ideas, like a mist hanging over a landscape. I like Ursula Le Guin's version of *Zhang 15* in her *Tao Te Ching* which expresses this beautifully:

Once upon a time
people who knew the Way
were subtle, spiritual, mysterious, penetrating,
unfathomable.

Since they're inexplicable

I can only say what they seemed like:
Cautious, oh yes, as if wading through a winter river.
Alert, as if afraid of the neighbours.
Polite and quiet, like houseguests.
Elusive, like melting ice.
Blank, like uncut wood.
Empty, like valleys.
Mysterious, oh yes, they were like troubled water.[10]

2.

The fundamental reason for the sages' gentle persuasion towards a mistrust of words was the belief that a frugal use of words was the best way to stay close to and thus, rooted in the silent unity of the Tao. ('Those who know don't talk; those who talk don't know.'[11]) The following passage is often quoted in Taoist writings and is attributed to Chuang Tzu, a contemporary of Confucius. It addresses this question of how far speech can take us and how we might, nonetheless, move beyond that boundary.

'The fish weir is the means to arrest a fish. Once one has caught the fish, one forgets about the fish weir. The snare is the means to arrest a hare. Once one has caught the hare, one forgets about the snare. Spoken words are the means to arrest a thought. Once one has caught the thinking, one forgets about the words. Where will I find a man who forgets about words to talk with him?'[12]

---

[10] Le Guin, Ursula, p.20

[11] Aldiss, Stephen

[12] Wagner, Rudolph G., p.31

When I first came upon these lines, I felt recognition and gratitude: all those centuries before Wittgenstein, this wise man found a way of summing up the relationship of words and that which lies beyond words. And then I reflected on the imagery, tried to enter it myself, starting with a sort of meditation on the construction of the 'weir'. It seemed to me that the more accurate and sympathetic the observation of the fish's behaviour became – that is, the closer the participation of the weir-maker's mind in the very being of the fish – the more subtle and refined would the weir become until it was, itself, a reflection of the light and slippery shadows of the moving, living fish. In a sense, the weir-maker would become one with the fish.

Over the years I continued to reflect on the corresponding relationship of words and 'thoughts', and, reaching further back in the metaphor, that of 'thoughts' and meanings which lie beyond even our thoughts: intuitions of the ineffable. I realized one day as I was turning it over in my mind that any 'fish' we might catch cannot be this ultimately 'empty', nameless 'fish' and I decided to call it the 'non-fish'.

3.

Before I came across Chuang Tzu and the fish-weir quote, another challenging and koan-like passage from a book of Native American writings had lodged in my mind. Whereas the 'Whereof' of fish-weirs and non-fish was paradoxical and intriguing, the following passage left me with a maddening and perhaps ultimately, unanswerable question. ('What is the Second Bush?') For me, the whole of this passage is extraordinary and could only have been written from within the tradition of the Native American concept of 'medicine' (a concept that I borrowed in the Miso Soup writings, above), which embraces a deep and seamless connection between Earth/Matter and Spirit. Learning how to participate consciously in this pre-existent connection (we are, willy-nilly, participants in it, if only blind and ignorant ones) – discovering what any one individual's part or place is in the Whole – is reflected in the practice of the Vision Quest, as well as in the rituals which shape daily tasks into acts of significance beyond their apparently more ordinary ends. Since everything material has a corresponding spiritual counterpart (and vice versa), consciously honouring one aspect will also and always mean its other aspect is honoured. For better or for worse, choosing what we honour and give more life or weight to is a serious business and learning how to make such choices is central to traditional teachings the world over.

'To make deer-hunting medicine, first you learn to see the bush that's in front of you, then the bush behind that bush, then the deer behind the bush behind the bush that's in front of you, then the spirit of that deer. Now you can call the deer, his spirit, and he'll walk up to you.'[13]

This passage worked inside me for years, puzzling me with its emphases on <u>learning</u> to see (how does that happen? Who is the teacher?) and on <u>two</u> bushes. I returned to it again and again, and it inhabited me – always there, someplace, in the

---

[13] eds. D. M. Dooling and Paul Jordan-Smith, p.52

back of my mind. It was not uncomfortable but it was insistent.

I thought the first bush was everything that we bring to a project – all our 'baggage' – and we won't be able to see anything as long as we're blinded by preconceptions, narratives, or ideas of gain. Thus, the first act must be to recognize our hopes and fears, desires – our 'projections' onto an imagined favourable outcome. In Buddhism the emphasis is placed on not being attached to outcome, or to any particular outcome. We cannot know how things will turn out, so we take the first step because it seems to be the best move that we can make, for now.

Identifying the first bush – or reflecting on what it might represent – appeared to be relatively uncomplicated. But the second bush? What was the second bush? As the months passed I learned that patience was clearly required, and steadfastness, in the face of frustration and confusion. I felt this waiting seemed not dissimilar to how I might have thought of prayer. Time passed and I continued to turn the question over and over in my mind, like polishing a pebble.

And then, several years later, without fanfare, but with a final message, the 'koan' of the Second Bush released me:
'The bush and I are I; there is no second bush.'

Part 5

'Between' is the word that most clearly identifies the event I have struggled to explain, to myself as well as to others. Martin Buber italicizes it – emphasizing it: 'Love does not cling to the *I* in such a way as to have the *Thou* only for its "content", its object; but love is *between I* and *Thou*.'[14] My body, the world around me, my thoughts and feelings, the bench I sit on, the bird that is singing, the rain, my mood – all of this becomes a 'Thou' – and the event – Beauty, Love – occurs *between* us, not just in me. Buber writes: 'The *Thou* meets me through grace – it is not found by seeking. But my speaking of the primary word (*I/Thou*) to it is an act of my being, is indeed *the* act of my being... Hence the relation means being chosen and choosing.'[15]

---

[14] Buber, Martin, p.11

[15] *ibid.*

Hard, Bitter Things

1.

Two hexagrams in the I Ching show situations in which something limitless, vast as the all-encompassing oceans of the earth, is either pouring into a too-small container – a lake or a pond – (something with limited capacity) or the limited container is being drained by the limitless. The first reflects a situation in which one feels flooded and overwhelmed (that an impossible amount is being asked of us, that we are bearing all the troubles of the world, that the To Do list is endless, infinite); the second, a situation where not only is the 'tank' empty, but it seems that no matter what one does to refill it, it just pours out the bottom: the tank is not only empty, it has a hole in it. Both situations are debilitating and dangerous and need to be addressed.

There are times when I feel 'beside myself', out of my skin, and the need is to re-establish connection and relationship, to lessen the distancing of Me/Not-Me or Us/Them. The ability to live life creatively and lovingly is an achievement that will always be touched by the experiences of being flooded and being drained. There is endless pain in the world – we can't contain it all and we can't solve it all. I can't take it all in and I can't make it all better.

2.

Events that have taken place at a distance or that, in spite of distance, implicate me can be as painful as those experiences which are more immediately and obviously part of my life. The first of the following writings was done shortly after the Boston Marathon bombings in 2013; the second, *Rare Earth*, in 2009 after I heard a radio programme about rare earth minerals. The third, *Riaño*, was written during a camping trip to the Picos de Europa when we found ourselves in a campsite above a huge dam and discovered that the original village of Riaño, along with neighbouring villages, was drowned beneath the waters of the reservoir after a period of great suffering and resistance on the part of all of the villagers in the area. I was angered on their behalf and moved by the stories which remained. A memorial to the villages and the men, women and children who had lived in them was erected high above the reservoir: 4 church bells – taken from the churches before they disappeared, and never rung subsequently – were set in apertures within 4 free-standing white walls which enclosed an empty space. This memorial was called El Silencio de Campanes.

3.

The death of a particular, dear friend was a life-changing event for me. Her final days were challenging and deeply moving. I include these three pieces from that time, and immediately after, to honour her and our friendship, for which I will always be grateful.

Part 6

Throughout the years of putting this material together, I have found myself searching for some way of understanding what the 'core' of the book is. The heart is the organ that pumps blood around the body; when it stops pumping, we die. The heart of this book, I came to recognize, after rediscovering Buber, circles around the *I/Thou* relationship – a relationship which has this understanding of 'heart' at its core. All the authors and poets that have inspired me speak of this dynamic directly or indirectly, when the *pulse* of Life and of *my* life is felt – suddenly and intensely – in what would otherwise be just a passing moment. They point to an experience of connection with oneself, with an object, with a moment, that is charged with mutuality, presence, transparency, grace, and I think 'presence' is the most important word in that list. If I am really present, then I am open and if I am open, then my heart is open. Standing on the edge of the moment, the 'I' disappears.

Iconography

1.

I was taught how to paint icons 20 years ago or so. I learned how to prepare the panel and the gesso, how to smooth the surface, establish the image, prepare the egg medium and the bole, how to gild and, finally, how to mix and apply the paint. During this lengthy process I learned how to prepare rabbit-skin glue to fix hessian to the panel, how to – patiently, patiently – lay coat after coat of warm gesso on the panel, first from side to side, then from top to bottom, then, again, from side to side, smoothing the final layer (maybe the 15th or 16th) until the texture of the finished surface glowed softly – milky and faultless – a texture of extraordinary beauty, almost impossible to describe. An icon is not an original work of art: it is as faithful a copy of an already existing, ancient image as possible. The time spent in the preparation and painting of the panel – weighing the ingredients on small brass scales, heating and cooling the solutions, grinding the pigments, applying bole and gold leaf, laying the paint on (thinly, thinly) – this time is like a prayer. An intense intimacy between oneself and the icon develops which can be almost unbearable at times. The tension between wanting to execute each delicate detail perfectly and the need to release any such desire, this tension itself must be patiently released again and again, until a quiet steady concentration is achieved, usually briefly. Painting an icon is an act of honouring the unknown, the ineffable, the sacred, the not-Me, or the non-Me but also honouring the unknown Me. In spite of the intricacy and demands of every step of the process, there is a great simplicity at the heart of the whole endeavour: it is not about me and what I can achieve at all; it's not about the intricacies and demands of life; instead it honours some quality of profound stillness which lies beyond one's ability to reproduce but which may, nonetheless, emerge and grace the work.

Orthodox churches in Greece are, of course, full of icons; no matter how tiny or isolated the chapel, there is always at least one, and usually many, icons whose gold glows warmly as one opens the door. Every island has its countless chapels named after saints familiar and unfamiliar – Aghios Giorgios, slaying his dragon from the back of his white horse; Aghia Paraskevi, solemnly holding a gold platter on which lie a pair of eyes; Aghios Eleftherios, Fanourios, Pantaleimon, Nikolaos, Sostis, Silviatros, Dimitrios; Aghia Kiriaki, Eleni, Varvara, Elousa. The names are the same on every island. On Lesbos, we reached Panayia Krifti by descending hundreds of rocky steps to a tiny cove where, carved into the rock of the cliffs was an even tinier room dedicated to the Hidden (Krifti) Virgin. The invariability of their imagery would seem to make it unlikely that icons could have a depth or an impact beyond their two-dimensionality, but they do have such an effect. I think it is that they, like the work of the alchemists, were created within a particular *temenos* or vessel of belief and intention. They are sacred objects, painted to reach beyond ordinary life, to offer a portal from ordinary life to a different realm – a spiritual, non-material realm. In American Indian cultures icons would be considered 'power' objects, 'medicine' objects connecting the earth and the earthly to the realm of the Great Spirit, the Ancestors. They offer a meaning and a hope of the significance of suffering, of witnessing, of fulfilling one's destiny, of something beyond the daily trials of life with its losses and challenges and sorrows.

The simplicity the Greek landscape and its villages is repeated throughout the islands and the mainland: the colours of sea, rock, and sky, of blinding white and brilliant blue chapels and churches, of bougainvillea; the scent of wild herbs, of fishing nets and fishing boats; the sounds of goat bells, as well as of mopeds and scooters. And the Greeks themselves, always talking, chatting, shouting, discussing, the older women still cheerfully in black, the men sitting inside or outside the *kafeinon*, playing backgammon or card games. This is not to understate or overlook the challenges and complexities of actual lives that are lived beyond these familiar representations, but rather to recognize and value how the land and the sea and time, itself, have shaped a theme and variations that echoes the relationship of surface to depth, of stillness to story that I have found in icons.

Lesbos (Half of the island was completely buried in ash following a catastrophic eruption 20 million years ago.)

2.

Grave Poetry – Delos – for drowned or shipwrecked sailors (Museum translations)

The entire small island of Delos – the navel of the Cyclades – is an ancient sanctuary dedicated to Apollo and Artemis. For more than a thousand years before the Greeks claimed it for their Gods, it existed as a sacred site. It was the most important pilgrimage site in the Aegean and to call its remains 'extensive' would be an understatement; it is breathtakingly vast, and excavations are still going on. There is a small museum on the island that manages to convey the astonishing vibrancy and variety of buildings and temples, market places and homes, devotional statues, columns, and tributes which would have covered the island as it maintained its dominance of trade in that area. Several of the famous – and beautiful – statues of lions which stood on either side of one of the main avenues are also part of the collection. But a small carved stone showing a boy trying to bail out his boat and the inscribed gravestones of drowned or shipwrecked individuals moved me most deeply. I copied four of these inscriptions down in my notebook, in the translations offered by the museum. Somehow the starkness of life for those who lived on the islands and traded on those treacherous and bountiful and beautiful waters transmitted itself in the words chosen in remembrance of lost children or friends.

3.

While present-day Delos is a silent and sun-bleached landscape covered with the white marble remains of ancient Delos, it is clear when one reads about the island and begins to imagine how it was at its peak, that it was a teeming, swarming centre of populations – both resident and transient – from far and wide. Hawkers of food and drink and of devotional statues or objects, which a pilgrim could pick up easily and leave as a tribute, slaves, merchants, inn-keepers, priests, individuals displaying sumptuous wealth (and others hoping to get it) would have crowded the streets, while ships and smaller craft filled the anchorage or tied up to piers. The atmosphere would have been intoxicating, overwhelming: a jostling, over-crowded, noisy, commercial, and, of course, sacred confusion of purposes and populations.

I thought that perhaps not much had changed as we sat waiting for our ferry. The ships have been replaced by skyscraping cruise liners and ferries, but the fishing boats are still there and the yachts of the fabulously wealthy are on display for those who stroll along the piers admiring them, as well as displaying their own 'riches' – clothes, children, grandchildren. Disembarking passengers are confronted by a wall of representatives from travel firms as well as by locals offering rooms or rides. And the sea and the sky, in all their changeableness, never change.

4.

There is often a sort of 'hangover' effect on returning from Greece, until the lens of familiarity is firmly back in place. Unexpectedly, I can find myself moving over that threshold still, seeing events and individuals 'in a different light'.

Gods among Us

The Ark

Every human body (including that
of the labourer, the fisherman, the shepherd
and the whore) is the ark
of the universe with its message[16]

In order to mix with mortals, for good or not-so-good reasons, Greek gods frequently disguised themselves, assuming a wide variety of forms. Each represented a particular quality of human nature in its unmediated state; they were powerful and numinous versions of *ourselves.* Sometimes I catch a glimpse of something in somebody – generally only in passing, almost always a stranger – and I say to myself, 'the Gods among us...' Nikiforos Vrettakos's small poem distils this experience into twenty-four perfectly chosen words. My reflections are lengthier.

---

[16]   Vrettakos, Nikiforos, p.59

5.

Finally, an encounter that moved me and reminded me of a piece of advice an elderly neighbour once offered me, as his father had offered it to him, to encourage persistence ('No problem baffles great zeal.')

Part 7

As tree rings register the year-upon-year growth of the original young, unbranched 'whip' and its 'heartwood', so the growth of *Benches* is registered in layers of learning and living and reflection upon the original moments and my notes. Those notes, or 'writings' have not been altered, not at the time and not thereafter (See 'Rough Edges'). Similarly, the subsequent attempts to gather and understand and introduce the original material have been allowed to carry their own 'signature' of where I was in my understanding and in my life, although the latter is only touched upon a few times. I might have chosen to put a date on each and every entry, but I didn't. The weaving together of experience, learning, and understanding, of inner and outer 'weather' takes place in ways we are unable to account for or explain. Our 'bark' expands to accommodate growth, occasionally almost splits, but unlike Eliot's 'shells' and 'husks' in *Little Gidding*, it remains fundamentally intact, becoming increasingly – and recognizably – individual.

Time and Tide

1.

I am a part of (and a participant in) the whole system in which I move and breathe, as sensitive to the weather and wind and barometric pressure and moon as the leaves on a tree or the tides, or the surface of a pond or a frisky horse. While we may choose to believe or act as if we are somehow separate from these all-encompassing systems, the truth is that our moods, the air we breathe, the fluids that circulate in our bodies, all are affected by what is going on around us, passing through us, entering us through our ears or nose or eyes or mouth or skin.

2.

Generally we are oblivious of the great forces and energies surging around or beneath us, invisible except in their results – the unimaginably huge and the unimaginably small, forces of creation and destruction. Like the surfers on Polzeath Beach, carrying their surfboards over a beach that looks like Picasso's *Guernica*, laughing and chatting to each other: we just don't register the evidence all around us. There are elemental forces that affect us at every moment and there are slow – gathering – forces that shape us over much longer periods of time, like a wave moving across the ocean.

3.

Quite a few years ago there was a television programme that featured a presenter who was not only knowledgeable about waves, but also deeply fascinated by them. He loved waves; they were the bearers of wonder and beauty and the interpreters of the mystery of life for him. The programme was life-enhancing.

Healing

Ring the bells that still can ring;
Forget your perfect offering;
There's a crack in everything;
It's how the light gets in.[17]

During the latter years covered by my writings I had two bad falls, the second just 6 months after the first. The road to physical recovery seemed straightforward, but it ended up involving me in much more than simply allowing time and exercise and rest to do the job. In the first week following the first fall, I received a book entitled *Wabi Sabi* – an extraordinary book, beautifully illustrated – impossible to categorize – that tells the simple story of a cat named Wabi Sabi who goes in search of enlightenment as to what her name means. The inscription at the start of the book reads, 'To providence hidden in tragic circumstances.' My circumstances weren't tragic, but the simplicity of the text, with each page containing a haiku verse, a collage, and a line of calligraphy nourished me deeply, and its gentle chronicling of the cat's journey, or pilgrimage, to find herself afforded me companionship. The story opens when Wabi Sabi's master is asked by 'visitors from another country' what her name means, Wabi Sabi awakens and waits to hear the answer: 'The cat's tail twitching, / she watches her master, still / waiting in

---

[17] Cohen, Leonard. *Anthem*

silence'.) 'That's hard to explain,'[18] comes the response. Wabi Sabi, her curiosity aroused, leaves the comfort of a home which had asked little of her and sets off to find the answer for herself.

The journey of healing begins with a change or a loss or a question which wakes us up, and we find we can't easily go back to sleep. Something that had been relatively comfortable and predictable/seamless – like my body or my routines – is unsettled, becomes, itself, questionable, sort of broken. Leonard Cohen's astonishing lines speak to the necessity for this to happen – for a 'crack' to be part of everything – in order for us to become enlightened. If there is no crack, or if the crack is somehow sealed over so quickly that it might as well not have existed, then we continue to sleep, in the dark of our unconsciousness.

(1-3)

The journey of healing – perhaps that's what our whole lives are – we all need it. Wounds come with life, with being alive, with being aware, conscious of our separateness and longing for 'home', for the experience of being held, contained, accompanied, beloved, significant: an indispensable part of something bigger than us. But without the challenge of a major loss, illness, or injury we may never need or choose to grow 'down' into the dark soil of our lives in order to stabilize or strengthen our roots, although aging and facing the end of life is likely to unsettle most of us to some degree.

---

[18]   Reibstein, Mark, p.2

*****

The slow process of physical healing, requiring that most precious commodity, time, offers the opportunity for embarking upon this journey, this pilgrimage, for a certain period. If we are as thorough as Wabi Sabi was in persevering with her search, her questioning, then in time we may find we are able to say 'thou' to our life and to the world we live in, and to feel its wholeness and its beauty. Each wound, each loss, each sense of our vulnerability gives us a piece of this journey because 'Thou' is an expression of non-separation, of a relationship that is indissoluble, even by death, least of all, by death.

* * * * *

(4)

A later, personal loss thrust me into an entirely new and strange and extraordinary place of loss and grief where my life was altered completely, but that also left me with a gift I could never have foreseen.

The first line of this piece refers to creatures and objects that appeared at particular moments, charged with a numinous significance, feeling like 'messengers'.

Return

Part I: Doing only what is necessary / Acting from a quiet place

Sometimes ideas and experiences that have become familiar over the years suddenly reveal another facet or dimension that was not previously glimpsed. For me, this occurred with the concept of 'Return'. I capitalize it because my first contact with it was in the I Ching where it is the name of Hexagram 24 (*Fu / Return.*). In the Wilhelm edition (1989 – now out of print), there are two ancient sayings: 'On the seventh day comes Return.'[19] and 'Return means coming back.' It seemed, from reflecting on these sayings and on further commentaries on the hexagram, that there were two possible meanings suggested for the word 'Return'. The first – emphasized in the text – was the *reappearance* of Life after a fallow period or season. (The hexagram is associated with winter and the solstice.) The second meaning, more elusive and less explicit, was concerned with the cessation of activity that *precedes* the reappearance, a 'return' to a state of rest. The second meaning carried an additional suggestion that it is in the nature of 'Heaven and Earth' to return, in this sense, to a state of rest and stillness periodically and regularly. And if something is in the nature of 'Heaven and Earth', then it is in human nature, as well.

Reading Rudolph Wagner's *Language, Ontology, and Political Philosophy in China* (sub-titled, *Wang Bi's Scholarly*

---

[19] Wilhelm, Richard, p.98

Exploration of the Dark (Xuanxue)), I was introduced to a much more profound understanding of *Fu* and its central importance in early Taoist philosophy. The Dark, the Nameless, the Source, the Root, the One: these were words that pointed to the 'place' of 'rest' advocated or delineated in the I Ching, the primal, ultimately unnameable, state to which Return led. 'Movement starts from rest as speech starts from silence, and both "return" to the original state.' (p.138). Return is thus to a state that is not representable. By its very nature it is neither yin nor yang, nor a combination of the two, as are the 64 hexagrams of the I Ching. In its hidden-ness it is empty of qualities and thus can only be suggested, pointed to.

Human beings are adaptable and restless – an uneasy mix – rarely at peace with ourselves or our lives. We wear ourselves out simply through not knowing when or how to stop, when or how to return to a state of rest and silence. George Herbert's wonderful poem, *The Pulley*, depicts God deciding which gifts he will bestow on his creature, Man. Having chosen to give strength, beauty, honour, pleasure, and wisdom, he hesitates: only one gift remains ungiven, and that is Rest. He decides to hold it back, so that when we finally experience a 'restlessnesse' for which no remedy is available in our human sphere, we will look to a different source: 'If goodnesse leade him not, yet wearinesse / May tosse him to my breast.' Again, it is the unconditioned, pre-existing unity which offers both rest and a new starting point. Without this 'turn' back towards where it all began – the Tao / the Source – we become more rest-less and weary, more likely to act impulsively, becoming unbalanced and reactive.

The Sage was considered to be the individual closest to this state, the primal condition, or Root, out of which the Yin and the Yang – and subsequently, the 10,000 things – arose. The Sage, being so intimately connected to the One, and to the underlying and immutable laws of Heaven and Earth, was seen as embodying a practical wisdom that was both profound and unadorned. Next to the Sage was the Emperor, and on down the list to those whose lives and instincts were at the mercy of those same 10,000 things.

The *Tao Te Ching* treats this idea over and over again from different angles. I began to recognize – in theory at least – that the closer I could align myself with even the idea of a state of rest and quiet (the Tao, the Way), the more likely it was that I wouldn't complicate my life and my communications with emotional spin-offs or misunderstandings.

I was quite preoccupied by these thoughts over several months and tried to put them into practice.

I began to appreciate how quickly we / I create more and more complexity. Because everything moves so fast, even when my response or reaction to a particular stimulus seems to me to be moderate, the tiniest spark can ignite a 'firestorm', either within my own psyche or in another person or situation. I made an effort to become more aware of the moment when I still had a choice, to ask myself, 'What is actually necessary here?' More often than not, it was for me to leave things as they were, to not try to 'fix' situations, to deal with my own unease by simply allowing it to be, by trusting in the movement of the Tao, or the natural flow of life within the person or situation.

* * * * *

Part II: *The Rainmaker* (An ancient narrative, here, in my words):

A certain area in China had not had any rain for a very long period and the drought had finally become so severe that the villagers decided to invite a Rainmaker to come and see if he could rectify the situation. A message was sent and he duly arrived. He chose to stay in a small hut on the edge of the village. He took his few possessions there and the wait began. He was seen to go out early with his wheelbarrow to fetch wood from the woodcutter, and a bit later, with his bucket, to draw water from the well. He swept the small area in front of the entry to the hut, and otherwise nobody saw him or heard anything. During the day smoke came out of the little pipe in the roof, and at night it was dark and quiet. On the 7th day it rained. The villagers came to thank the Rainmaker and to ask him what he had done. He told them all he had done was that which was necessary to his simple existence, nothing more: to fetch wood and water when needed, to rest when it was dark, and to care for the little hut. By returning to the roots of life, he created (or recreated), the balance that had been lost.

Part III: 'Yet'...

The vastness of C. G. Jung's research into the human mind, spirit, and soul is almost incomprehensible. A lifetime of driven dedication to exploring and seeking to understand the depths of our ancient psyche and its modern incarnation yielded collected works that extend to 20 volumes, and that does not include the most personal and private work – on his own psychic evolution and its manifestations – recorded and reflected in his extraordinary paintings. Yet, when it came to his final thoughts, which reached the world through the [possibly semi-] autobiographical work, *Memories, Dreams, Reflections*, Jung expressed something which on first reading seems melancholic, if not disillusioned, certainly confused:

'*When Lao-tzu* (the 'author' of the *Tao Te Ching*) *says, 'All are clear, I alone am clouded,' he is expressing what I now feel in advanced old age. Lao-tzu is the example of a man with superior insight who has seen and experienced worth and worthlessness, and who at the end of his life desires to return into his own being, into the eternal unknowable meaning... This is old age and a limitation. Yet there is so much that fills me: plants, animals, clouds, day and night, and the eternal in man. The more uncertain I have felt about myself, the more there has grown up in me a feeling of kinship with all things. In fact it seems to me as if that alienation which so long separated me from the world has become transferred into my own inner world, and has revealed to me an unexpected unfamiliarity with myself.*'[20]

On a more subtle reading, Jung seems to be feeling his way into an experience that is the opposite of the 'limitation', which he ascribes to old age: he is describing something

---

[20] Jung, C. G., p.393

'other', and his use of the word, 'Yet', speaks to this turn away from those conventional expectations of old age. Then follows an incredibly beautiful phrase: '*Yet there is so much that fills me: plants, animals, clouds, day and night, and the eternal in man.*'

It is as if a breath which has been held for a long time is finally released and a sense of expansiveness and grace is experienced: '*...there has grown up in me a feeling of kinship with all things.*'

This turn away from previous expectations, conventional expectations of old age, involves allowing the 'self' we know to slip away, the self that has furnished our identity throughout life. Whatever sense of self-control or self-reliance or self-knowledge we have had is of little use at the end of life. But is there anything else to comfort us? Anything to turn towards, or return to? Asking the question opens a space: if we knock on a door – even imaginatively – there is already implied the possibility that beyond the door there is another space. '*Yet...*' can be the threshold over which we step into that space, but first, we must release the self we've known and turn towards the unknown for a new beginning.

* * * * *

At the deepest level, I find I know less and less about myself, while, at the same time, I am becoming more and more familiar with a space in which this 'myself' can just be trusted to go on being, without form. I have repeatedly found myself at the point where every thought or feeling or sensation that I track or think of as Me or Mine falls away and I not only do not know *who* I am, I don't know *what* I am, or what anybody or anything else is either. All qualities dissipate, all forms dissolve and there is just this light-in-all-things, this vibrancy of flow. The need or impulse to 'know' evaporates with this recognition and my appreciation of life in all its forms, visible and invisible, expands and softens. We are connected by this vast unknowability, and, out of that recognition, a 'feeling of kinship with all things' can arise.

And when I blink myself back into Here and Now the forms reassemble themselves into their familiar worldly shapes, their qualities intact, but I can still sense my and their formless energy presence.

Kaleidoscope

1.

According to Wikipedia, the etymology of 'kaleidoscope' arises from three Greek words which, taken together, translate as 'The observation of beautiful forms'. The kaleidoscopes that I was familiar with as a child consisted of a cylinder containing pieces of brightly coloured glass in one end that fell into different patterns when a cuff on that end was turned by the viewer who was peering in through a small window on the other end.

On a snowy afternoon I observed a looping sort of dance taking place in front of me, and each of its elements evoked scenes from years extending back from the present into my childhood: sledges, snow, running dogs, laughs, tumbles, screams – an unchanging winter panorama. This observation was affectionate, compassionate, and linked not only the actual generations, but also the 'inner' ages of Me. Rather than envy, I felt an identification with the younger generation – *I* did that, too; *I* know what that feels like. It was a joyful, if quiet sort of feeling.

Erik Erikson was one of the first (barring Shakespeare) to really explore the stages of life, and *generativity* was the quality he identified with the last stage. This term described the capacity and willingness to support, encourage, and enjoy the younger generation's growth and movement into positions of power and authority and responsibility, even if it meant being ousted by such a move! Allowing the young to take over. Recently I heard a conversation recorded for radio between two elderly men: 'It's good that we die,' one said, 'we are full of all of *our* ideas or stories which were the scripts and narratives we grew up with; they need to die so that new words, ideas, narratives can take their place.' This seemed to be about trusting life – letting go, releasing, trusting the seeds and the seasons. Not even about trusting we have passed on enough... simply trusting Life and those who follow us.

However, a slightly melancholy note is also present in the piece around what we see and don't see of each other, what we can only know when we arrive at the same place as our parents and grandparents. People see an old-lady-Me, and that's what I *am*, not what I *was*, not how I experience myself from inside, but that's how it is – you only learn through experience.

2.

Cafe Hollyhock: A small cafe in Richmond's Terrace Gardens offering outside tables that look down over sloping gardens to the Thames. On a winter's day I arrived with some Christmas presents (a 'cinnamon box') and a few purchases from a health food store ('black sunflower seeds') and sat on the narrow porch where a robin was pecking around for crumbs and below me children were sledding on the short, moderately steep slope below the cafe. Following this tea pause I had made my way to a nearby plant nursery and then entered Richmond Park where a much longer, steeper, and wider hill was teeming with families and dogs making the most of frozen ground with an inch or so of snow-cover.

3.

Like an endless barn dance where partners are swapped around and the participants weave around each other repeating the same steps with different partners, the turning of Life creates different patterns from the same 'pieces' and I was grateful as well as a little rueful about my inclusion in this shared generational 'dance'. The next piece was a bit different in that it arose from a felt connection between a particular moment, and its content, that had occurred long ago and a moment in the present that might have simply followed the previous one, evolved out of it, were it not for the passage of twenty years or more. Whereas 'Cafe Hollyhock' reflected a direct, almost physical connection over time between generations, this piece connected me to myself, to my own mind and to a remembered intimacy with the 'fabric' of space, the recognition of how, for me, space had had and still had a sensual quality to it that I could see and hear and feel. The new recognition also suggested a shift in the focus of this recognition to make it more inclusive.

4.

One of those moments when the sheer number of years that have passed in one's life between a remembered event and its reminder in the present – its echo – is recognized with a sense of shock.

Acknowledgements

I am grateful to Faber and Faber Ltd, publishers, for permission to reproduce *Postscript*, from *The Spirit Level* by Seamus Heaney.

I am also grateful to Faber and Faber, Ltd, publishers, for permission to reproduce an excerpt from *Little Gidding*, from *Four Quartets* by T. S. Eliot.

© Buber, Martin, 2016, *I and Thou*. Excerpt reprinted with permission of T & T, an imprint of Bloomsbury Publishing Plc.

Excerpt from *Memories, Dreams, Reflections* reprinted by permission of HarperCollins Publishers Ltd. © C. G. Jung, 1995.

I am grateful to Imperfect Publishing for permission to reproduce an excerpt from *Wabi-Sabi: For Artists, Designers, Poets & Philosophers* by Leonard Koren.

Excerpt from Lao Tzu, *Tao Te Ching: A New English Version*, by Ursula K. Le Guin. © 1997 by Ursula K. LeGuin. Reprinted by arrangement with The Permissions Company, Inc., on behalf of Shambhala Publications Inc., Boulder, Colorado, www.shambhala.com.

Just Now, by Samuel Menashe, © 1971, 1973, 2004, 2005 by Samuel Menashe. Reprinted by permission of the Library of America, New York, N.Y., www.loa.org. All rights reserved.

I am grateful to the State University of New York Press for suggesting I utilize 'Fair Use' in the reprinting of material from *Language, Ontology, and Political Philosophy in China*, by Rudolf G. Wagner.

I am utilizing Fair Use in including the following material:

The first verse of Leonard Cohen's *Anthem*. The copyright is held by Sony/ATV.

The passages from the *SUNY* publication by Rudolph Wagner, with the permission of the publishers.

The poem, *The Ark*, permission for which I have sought but have had no reply from the publishers.

The 10-word extract from the Hackett publication, *Tao te ching/Lao-tzu*.

The extract *Deer-hunting Medicine* from the Parabola Books publication, *I Become Part of It*. I have applied for permission but have been unable to trace the publishers.

The 12-word extract from the Penguin Arkana publication, *I Ching or Book of Changes*.

Extracts from *Wabi Sabi* are reproduced with the permission of Hachette Children's Books, publishers.

The cover image and photograph accompanying the text on page 12 show a willow sculpture by Julia Clarke installed in Kew Gardens in 2017.

Personal Acknowledgements

I am extremely grateful to friends, family, and colleagues who read versions of *Benches* as it evolved. In particular, Will Frank, Sue Schwartz, Anne Young, Martin Kelly, Deirdre McConnell, Trish Perry, Anne Day-Jones, and Janie Grimes. Special thanks to Christopher Perry whose thoughtful reading and detailed response deepened my own engagement with the material. And finally, to my husband, Hugh, for his loving and unfailing support, as always.

Bibliography

Aldiss, Stephen. *Tao Te Ching / Lao-Tzu.* Hackett Publishing Company, Inc., Indianapolis, Indiana, 1993.

Buber, Martin. *I and Thou.* Bloomsbury Academic, London, 2016.

Dooling, D. M. and Jordan-Smith, Paul (Eds.). *I Become Part of It: Sacred Dimensions in Native American Life.* Parabola Books, New York, 2004.

Edinger, Edward F., *Anatomy of the Psyche: Alchemical Symbolism in Psychotherapy.* Open Court Publishing Company, La Salle, Illinois, 1993. (J. B. Priestley's vision, p. 14 of 'Benches')

Eliot, T. S., *Collected Poems 1909-1962.* Faber and Faber, London, 1983.

Heaney, Seamus. *The Spirit Level.* Faber and Faber. London, 1996.

Herbert, George. *A Choice of George Herbert's Verse.* Faber and Faber. London. 1981. ('The Pulley')

Jung, C. G.. *Memories, Dreams, Reflections.* Fontana Press. London.1995.

Koren, Leonard. *Wabi-Sabi for Artists, Designers, Poets & Philosophers.* Imperfect Publishing, Point Reyes, California, 2008.

Le Guin, Ursula. *Lao Tzu: A Book about the Way and the Power of the Way*. Shambhala, Boston and London, 1998.

Menashe, Samuel. *New & Selected Poems*. Ed. Christopher Ricks. Bloodaxe Books, Tarset, Northumberland, UK, 2010.

Reibstein, Mark. *Wabi Sabi*. Little Brown and Company (Hatchette Book Group USA), New York, Boston, 2008.

Vrettakos, Nikiforos. *Selected Poems*. Trans. David Connelly. AIORA Press, Athens, 2015.

Wagner, Rudolf G.. *Language, Ontology, and Political Philosophy in China: Wang Bi's Scholarly Exploration of the Dark (Xuanxue)*. State University of New York Press, Albany, 2003.

Wilhelm, Richard. Trans. Cary F. Baynes. *I Ching or Book of Changes*. Penguin (Arkana), London, 1989.

PRINTED AND BOUND BY:

Copytech (UK) Limited trading as Printondemand-worldwide,
9 Culley Court, Bakewell Road, Orton Southgate.
Peterborough, PE2 6XD, United Kingdom.